A. Christiano

SO-BNK-070

THE RHETORIC OF AGITATION AND CONTROL

THE RHETORIC OF AGITATION AND CONTROL

John Waite Bowers and **Donovan J. Ochs**
University of Colorado   *University of Iowa*

WAVELAND

PRESS, INC.

Prospect Heights, Illinois

For information about this book, write or call:
Waveland Press, Inc.
P.O. Box 400
Prospect Heights, Illinois 60070
(708) 634-0081

Copyright © 1971 by John W. Bowers and Donovan J. Ochs
1991 reissued by Waveland Press, Inc.

ISBN 0-88133-580-0

All rights reserved. No part of this book may be reproduced, stored in a retrieval system, or transmitted in any form or by any means without permission in writing from the publisher.

Printed in the United States of America

7 6 5 4 3 2 1

PREFACE

This is not a handbook for rebellion. It is designed to provide the basis for understanding the instrumental and symbolic acts performed in the service of agitation and control. It is theory, and the application of that theory is intellectual.

After reading the book, the student should be able to specify rather precisely the rhetorical ingredients used by agitators and establishments in their recipes for social change and social control. He should have assimilated a frame of reference that, if used habitually, will sharpen his analytic skills. Finally, he should be able to predict, within reasonable limits, the outcomes of agitational events as they occur.

Iowa City, Iowa   J. W. B.
October 1970   D. J. O.

ACKNOWLEDGMENTS

Our greatest debt is to students in the course, "The Rhetoric of Agitation and Control," at the University of Iowa. They suffered through the book's early drafts, often supplied valuable illustrations, and took delight in reacting critically. Graduate students and faculty in rhetoric, public address, and communication research at Iowa forced us to rethink and adjust many of our claims. The faculty and students in the Department of Rhetoric at the University of California, Davis, served as an early critical and responsive audience for several chapters. Professor Robert Scott's careful commentary was invaluable.

Substantively, we owe a great deal to the various task forces of the National Commission on the Causes and Prevention of Violence. The reports submitted by these task forces to the Commission are models of careful research, and they have contributed heavily to this book.

CONTENTS

Chapter one

RHETORIC, AGITATION AND CONTROL, AND SOCIAL CHANGE

In a broad sense, this book is concerned with analyzing the process of social change. It investigates the possibilities for understanding the causes and the consequences of the fascinating human behaviors called agitation and control. It therefore applies some generalizations and methods from the disciplines of psychology, sociology, political science, and history.

In a narrower sense, the book is about the *rhetoric* of the social phenomena we call agitation and control. As rhetoricians, we are centrally concerned with the messages generated by the participants in social-change movements. From our point of view, the causes and consequences of these messages—the psychological, sociological, political, and historical aspects—are crucial, but secondary. In this chapter, we shall define the important terms (rhetoric, agitation, and control) and place them in a frame of social research.

What Is Rhetoric?

Most definitions of rhetoric specify that it is a theory or a rationale or an art (in the sense that "art" refers to a set of principles), that it has to do with persuasion, and that it is limited to verbal phenomena. Our definition is in the spirit of the traditional ones, though it extends their scope. We define rhetoric as *the rationale of instrumental, symbolic behavior.*

A message or other act is *instrumental* if it contributes to the production of another message or act. For example, an infant's crying is instrumental in persuading its mother that she should change its diaper or relieve its discomfort. The mother's rhythmic patting of the infant's back is instrumental in achieving a release of gas from its stomach. The student's essay is instrumental in persuading a teacher to assign a grade of *A*. The politician's speech is instrumental in persuading his colleagues that they should vote for a bill and/or in persuading his constituents that they should vote for him in the next election.

Instrumental behavior can be distinguished from *expressive* behavior and *consummatory* behavior. Behavior is expressive if it neither intends to produce nor succeeds in producing any social consequences. The infant's cooing in the absence of any other person is expressive. The carpenter's exclamation when he strikes his thumb with a hammer is expressive. Behavior is consummatory if it is the final step in satisfying a need, if no other behavior is necessary to satisfy that need. The infant's burp is consummatory. The teacher's assignment of a grade is consummatory. The constituent's vote is consummatory.

In this book, we frequently distinguish between rhetorical statements and ideological statements. We define ideological statements as being expressive of a set of values and beliefs rather than being instrumental. A strictly ideological statement is not made to persuade or to alter behavior. It is made to define the position of an individual or group. In practice, of course, most statements share ideological and rhetorical functions. We might define "spinach is good" as an ideological statement and "spinach is good so you should eat it" as a rhetorical statement. But it can be successfully maintained that the ideological statement in most contexts implies the rhetorical one. Purely expressive statements are rare.

Behavior is *symbolic* if it has a referential function—if it stands for something else. Verbal behavior, whether descriptive or persuasive, is almost completely symbolic. No natural or necessary connection exists between sounds produced in speech, squiggles produced in writing, and the real world. Words used instrumentally, therefore, are clearly in the purview of rhetoric.

We think, however, that many kinds of nonverbal behavior are also symbolic and therefore appropriate to rhetorical analysis. We find it useful to imagine a continuum of symbolic behavior. On one end of the continuum are words and other kinds of *arbitrarily* symbolic behavior, behavior for which no natural connection exists with what the behavior stands for, the referent. On the other end of the continuum is more *naturally* symbolic behavior, behavior in which the observer need go through no arbitrary set of rules to establish the relationship between the sign and its referent. If an agitator says to an establishment spokesman, "You are disgusting, like urine," he is using arbitrarily symbolic behavior that must be decoded by the application of the rules of syntax and semantics. If, instead, he throws at the establishment spokesman a plastic bag filled with urine, he is using more naturally symbolic behavior. We consider both kinds of behavior symbolic, since they stand for general concepts that an observer easily infers.

This definition of rhetoric applies to any situation in which persuasion occurs or is intended to occur. We must now circumscribe more specifically the rhetorical situations for which this book provides theory and analyses.

Agitation and Control

A traditional definition of "agitation" would read something like this: Agitation is persistent, long-term advocacy of a social change, where resistance to the change is also persistent and long-term. This definition makes possible the inclusion under the term "agitators" of such rhetorical practitioners as William Wilberforce, whose cause was to eliminate the British slave trade; John Bright and Richard Cobden, whose cause was to eliminate the British Corn Laws; and William Lloyd Garrison, whose cause was to eliminate slavery in America.

Another traditional definition might be: Agitation is a style of persuasion characterized by highly emotional argument based on citation of grievances and alleged violation of moral principles. Under this definition could come such "agitators" as Patrick Henry and Samuel Adams (the American Revolution) and Joseph McCarthy (anti-communism in the United States).

Both definitions are problematical, though they may be useful for some purposes. The first definition does not succeed in distinguishing agitation from other forms of rhetorical practice, except in the matter of persistence. Hence it fails to establish agitation as a special kind of persuasion in any significant sense. The second definition includes such terms as "highly emotional" and "moral principles." These terms themselves all but defy definition. Each definition of agitation would include some practitioners excluded by the other, since persistence, emotionality, and moral principles are not necessarily coterminous.

We have chosen to devise a new definition of "agitation" rather than attempt to adjust the old ones. Our definition is: *Agitation exists when* (1) *people outside the normal decision-making establishment* (2) *advocate significant social change and* (3) *encounter a degree of resistance within the establishment such as to require more than the normal discursive means of persuasion. Control refers to the response of the decision-making establishment to agitation.*

This definition has the virtue of clearly delineating a certain kind of rhetorical situation as agitational. It has the further virtue of defining agitation in a way that requires interaction between two social groups rather than as a characteristic of a certain kind of persuasive attempt or a certain kind of persuader. Its only shortcoming, as far as we can tell, is that it excludes some practitioners who have traditionally been called agitators.

People outside the normal decision-making establishment

The notion of an establishment is, of course, a relative one. In some social organizations, the establishment is an individual, as, for example, the autocratic father of a family, or the Pope speaking *ex cathedra*. In most social organizations, the establishment is a small group of decision-makers in which resides the legitimate power of the organization. This power has two parts: (1) *legislation*, the power of deciding policy; and (2) *enforcement*, the power of administering negative and positive sanctions to those who violate and observe the policies, respectively. These two functions of an establishment may be performed by the same group or by different groups.

Whether an individual is inside or outside the establishment depends on the nature of the organization and the issue at conflict. In a family, for example, the father may be the establishment where use of the automobile is concerned. A son, refused the use of the automobile, would be in a position in which he might agitate against the father, for the son would be outside the establishment. In the same family, the mother might decide on the main course for dinner by majority vote. A daughter, loser in the vote, would not be in a position to agitate, using our definition, since she is a part of the legislative establishment.

Similarly, in more substantive affairs, we do not classify as agitators those who attempt to persuade within the establishment, no matter what style they use in their persuasion attempts. According to our definition, Joseph McCarthy was not an agitator when he carried on his anti-communist hearings, nor was Eugene McCarthy when he served in an anti-administration capacity in the Senate and when he pursued the Democratic presidential nomination. Neither were John Bright and Richard Cobden when they argued in Parliament against the British Corn Laws. This is not to say that such dissenting members of the establishment have no role in agitation. Sometimes, as we shall see in later chapters, agitation movements are deeply affected by them.

Significant social change

Social change is any change, written or unwritten, in the way society regulates itself. Such a change may be substantive (e.g., higher wages for mine workers) or procedural (e.g., a collective bargaining system for mine workers). It may be concerned with the use of power or the distribution of power. It may affect one group, many groups, or all groups in a culture. It may be political, religious, economic, or all of these things. It may require enactment of legislation or repeal of legislation. It may imply bigger government, smaller government, or no government. All these things are matters of ideology.

"Significant" is a difficult word to define. It is something like "taste," for it has no direct real-world referent. To define an object or event as "significant," one must pass from it, through an individual's value system, and out again with a tag like "yes," "no," "don't know," or "maybe." If the boy we referred to earlier decides to agitate for the family car, he probably would consider the cause significant, but the rest of us probably would not. The rest of us can usually agree, however, that some social changes having wide-ranging consequences *are* significant. We shall let the definition go at that, assuming that the social changes advocated in the cases dealt with in this book are consequential enough to be considered significant.

Resistance such as to require more than the normal discursive means of persuasion

This element in our definition is our most radical departure from traditional definitions of agitation. We think that the central element in a persuasive attempt, if we are to call it agitation, should be the exercise of extra-discursive means of persuasion. Most other treatments of the subject are analyses of speeches and essays. Some of these are excellent analyses, but in our judgment something more is required for the understanding of agitational rhetoric. Hence we have made our primary concern the analysis of instrumental, symbolic events that are largely nonverbal, or extraverbal. We are interested in speeches and essays because of the insight they give us about the ideologies of agitating groups, but we consider other things more central to the agitation itself.

We say that agitation exists, then, when a movement for significant social change from outside the establishment meets such resistance within the establishment that more than the normal discursive means of persuasion occur. This definition excludes from agitation individuals and groups who never go beyond the normal discursive means of persuasion, although such individuals and groups almost invariably interact with agitating groups for similar goals. Hence, for example, in eighteenth-century England, the Chartists, an agitating group, worked against the Corn Laws concurrently with the non-agitating anti-Corn Law League. In the United States in 1968, the Coalition for an Open Convention, largely a non-agitating group, worked concurrently with the Yippies and the Mobilization Committee to End the War in Vietnam, both agitating groups. Such organizations as the League of Women Voters, the Americans for Democratic Action, and the American Civil Liberties Union often work toward the same goals as agitating groups, but employ only discursive means of persuasion. According to our definition, such groups, when they dissent from the establishment, are not agitators. The study of the rhetoric of agitation and control—as the cases in this book and many others illustrate—has enough scope without including every instance of protest.

Why does agitation occur?

The social antecedents of agitation are relevant, though not crucial, to a rhetorical analysis. According to Kenneth E. Boulding:

> Protest [for which we would read "agitation"] arises when there is strongly felt dissatisfaction with existing programs and policies of government or other organizations [for which we would read "establishments"], on the part of those who feel themselves affected by these policies but who are unable to express their discontent through regular and legitimate channels, and who feel unable to exercise the weight to which they think they are entitled in the decision-making process. When nobody is listening to us and we feel we have something to say, then comes the urge to shout.[1]

In short, agitation occurs when a group has a grievance or grievances and no remedy in what Hans Toch calls "the more common resources of the social order."[2]

Two kinds of agitation

We have already referred to the necessity of an understanding of ideology as prerequisite to the understanding of a particular agitation. One distinction among ideologies will be especially useful to us in our attempt to analyze the interactions among agitators and establishments. As labels for these kinds of ideologies, we shall use the terms *agitation based on vertical deviance* and *agitation based on lateral deviance*. Agitation based on vertical deviance occurs when the agitators subscribe to the value system of the establishment, but dispute the distribution of benefits or power within that value system. Agitation based on lateral deviance occurs when the agitators dispute the value system itself.

John Robert Howard, in "The Flowering of the Hippie Movement," explains and illustrates the distinction:

> Vertical deviance occurs when persons in a subordinate rank attempt to enjoy the privileges and prerogatives of those in superior rank. Thus, the ten-year-old who sneaks behind the garage to smoke is engaging in . . . vertical deviance, as is the fourteen-year-old who drives . . . despite being too young . . . and the sixteen-year-old who bribes a twenty-two-year-old to buy him a six-pack of beer. . . .
>
> Lateral deviance occurs in a context in which the values of the non-deviant are rejected. The pot-smoking seventeen-year-old, wearing Benjamin Franklin eyeglasses and an earring, does not share his parents' definition of the good life. Whereas value consensus characterizes vertical deviance, there is a certain kind of value dissensus involved in lateral deviance.[3]

If the term "the establishment" is substituted for "those in superior rank," the application to agitation and control is direct.

Agitations based on vertical deviance are likely to be relatively direct and easily understood ideologically. The American labor movement agitations, except for a few early and unsuccessful elements, are characterized by vertical deviance. The worker and employer agree that high wages, job security, and ample leisure are valuable commodities. The question being agitated is: How shall these emoluments be distributed in the system? As lateral deviance of the agitators from the establishment increases, so does ideological and agitational complexity. As we shall show later, some of the agitators at the Democratic National Convention in 1968 rejected not only the policies and personnel of the Democratic party, but also the value of the party itself and of the entire American political and economic system. This wide lateral deviance had its effects on the nature and extent of the agitation.

The nature of an agitation based on vertical deviance is likely to be "hot," to use Marshall McLuhan's term.[4] The issues, because they are based on a single value system, are easy to understand, and the aim of the agitator is to win support by making his case as clearly as possible. An agitation based on vertical deviance will end as soon as the establishment makes the appropriate concessions, concessions to demands that are explicit, realistic, and publicly available.

An agitation based on lateral deviance, on the other hand, is likely to employ "cool" strategies. The agitators' ideology and demands are difficult to understand, and the agitators are likely to display symbols, engineer events, and behave in ambiguous ways. Their rationale is that the public, whose support they would like to have, will feel such a strong need to understand agitative symbols, events, and behavior that they will supply the missing information and explanations themselves. One agitation based on lateral deviance was that carried out by the Yippies at the 1968 Democratic National Convention. The rationale for the Yippie demonstrations was expressed in the *New York Free Press*: "We put a finger up their ass and tell them, 'I ain't telling you what I want,' then they got a problem." [5] This is "cool" agitation.

Given these basic and rather general definitions of agitation and control, an analysis of some of the more important psychological and sociological phenomena which occur in the process of social change is possible. Our particular focus will be on the concepts *social organization, power,* and *rumor.*

Social Change

Social organization

Almost every writer on social organization uses the family as his primary example, and we shall not be exceptions. Imagine a family of five: father, mother, teen-age son, teen-age daughter, and subteen daughter. In this section, we shall focus on two aspects that this miniature social organization shares with others: *structure* and *goal orientation.* The third principal characteristic, *power,* we shall reserve for the next section.

The family is *structured*. It has a set of *procedures* by which decisions are made and a set of *positions* in which decision-making power rests. That is to say, in the typical contemporary American family, the father and mother are the decision-making *establishment*. The family's structure invests them with *control*, with final decisional authority. The locus of the establishment may shift from one parent to the other or be shared in some way, depending on the kind of decision to be made. In many families, the father has ultimate control over task and property decisions, while the mother is the establishment for socio-emotional decisions. That is, the father usually decides where the family will live, how and on what it will spend money, and who will do the necessary jobs within the family. The mother usually decides with whom the family will socialize and how best to raise and provide affection for the members of the family. The children's stake in this establishment may be large or small. If important decisions are made by majority vote, their role is relatively important; if those decisions are handed down by the establishment, the children are literally disenfranchised. Any member of the family who disapproves of a particular decision in which he did not actively participate is a potential agitator.

The complexity of the establishment in social organizations depends on its size and its functions. We know of no family, for example, that has annual elections, a constitution, by-laws, and committee meetings. On the other hand, a University of California is inconceivable *without* its governor, regents, president, chancellors, deans, committee chairmen, and memo-routing slips.

Equally obvious is another characteristic of every social organization, including our hypothetical family: *goal orientation*. Every organization has a set of expressed or implied purposes. Some such purposes are: simple self-perpetuation; maintenance of a value system; gathering information; disseminating information; enlarging the base of support and power; policy-making; policy implementation; enforcement of policy; and the like. The possibility of successfully overcoming the establishment in any organization depends, of course, on its function. In the family, the goal of self-perpetuation is thwarted when a sufficient number of members leave home. The goal of maintaining a value system is not achieved if the children reject the parents' system. To thwart other goals requires other measures, one of which may be agitation.

The organization's goal orientation may be expressed in a coherent set of fact and value statements. When it is, we say that the group has an *ideology*—a set of statements which define the unique characteristics of the organization and express the unique set of beliefs to which the members theoretically subscribe. Their subscription is theoretical because members often belong to organizations in name only. In the family, for example, one set of ideological statements might require the members to believe in the tenets of a particular religion. The teen-age son might internally reject those tenets, but continue to attend Sunday Mass in order to enjoy the benefits of belonging to his family, e.g., meals, housing, and transportation.

Bases of social power

Besides structure and goal orientation, social organizations have in common a distribution of social power. One individual has power over another when he can influence the other's behavior. Changes in the distribution of this power, we believe, are the main goals of most agitating groups. Hence an understanding of the phenomenon is crucial to an understanding of the rhetoric of agitation and control.

Some preliminary generalizations about power, supported by research, are: (1) The need for social power of one kind or another is a nearly universal attribute of people in Western culture. (2) An individual or a group seldom gives up power voluntarily to another individual or group. (3) The exercise of social power is satisfying *in itself* to most individuals in Western culture.

John R. P. French, Jr., and Bertram Raven have analyzed the types of social power.[6] We shall summarize their analysis and add a few qualifying notes.

French and Raven perceive five distinguishable types of social power. They are: *reward* power, *coercive* power, *legitimate* power, *referent* power, and *expert* power.

One individual or group has *reward power* over another when the first can give rewards to the second. The more rewards the first can give, the more the second is under the influence of reward power. Rewards can be of two types: (1) the giving of positively perceived things and events, and (2) the withdrawal of negatively perceived things and events. For example, in our hypothetical family the father may persuade his subteen daughter that she should do her homework by promising her a movie (giving) or suspending a rule about bedtime (withdrawal).

Coercive power exists when one individual or group is able to influence another's behavior by the threat of punishment. A person who has coercive power, in effect, says to the influencee: "Do as I say or I will deprive you of something you have or prevent you from getting something you want."

Legitimate power—French and Raven's third type—is somewhat more complicated than the others. It exists when one individual or group is perceived by another as having a sort of charter or social contract, an assigned position, through which that individual or group can exert influence. Its potency depends on the degree to which the influencee has accepted the authority system of the particular organization. In every organization, the establishment holds legitimate power, and this characteristic is a defining one for the establishment. Thus, for example, parents have legitimate power in the family; the hierarchy has legitimate power in the Catholic church; the government holds legitimate power in the state. These agencies are also the establishments of those organizations.

One individual or group has *referent power* over another when the influencee is attracted to and identifies with that individual or group. The power comes from the strong desirability of a personal relationship for the influencee with the attracting agency. Although French and Raven do not note the phenomenon, negative referent power can also exist. That is, if the individual or group repels the influencee, he is likely to oppose the direction of influence which the repelling agency expresses. Thus, for example, in 1969 Senator Strom Thurmond of South Carolina, in an attempt to exert negative referent power on liberals in the United States, is supposed to have expressed a desire for one candidate for the United States Supreme Court when he actually favored another. Similarly, if the parents in our hypothetical family appear to endorse one of the teen-age daughter's beaux, they might find that they have exercised negative referent power.

Finally, *expert power* exists when one individual or group thinks that another has superior knowledge or skill in a particular area in which influence is to be exerted. When a client goes for advice to a psychotherapist or clergyman or lawyer he is requesting the exercise of expert power. Insofar as teachers influence their students' behavior in the teachers' areas of specialized knowledge, the influence probably results from expert power.

French and Raven's analysis needs to be qualified in certain ways. Rather clearly, all the five bases can be reduced to reward and coercive (punishment) power. When an individual succumbs to legitimate power, he does so because he perceives negative consequences if he does not and/or positive consequences if he does. That is, we stop our cars at stop signs to avoid paying a traffic fine as well as to obey legitimate authority. An individual succumbs to referent power because the prospect of a personal relationship is positively reinforcing (rewarding) for him or the expectation of losing such a relationship is punishing. Similarly, expert power depends on the influencee's perception that following an expert's advice will maximize his rewards and minimize his punishments.

In a situation of agitation and control, we believe that power is likely to be distributed in this way: (1) The establishment always controls legitimate power. This is so by definition. However, we think that legitimate power, by itself, is always insufficient to maintain an establishment in its position of control. (2) The establishment also normally is capable of exerting coercive power. Only rarely does an agitation group have coercive power, even for its own members. The state, however, can imprison people and make war on them. The administration can fire people. The church can excommunicate. Establishments can always withhold from individual members the use of the organization's resources. The parent, for example, can refuse the use of the family car. (3) Both the establishment and the agitators have some reward power. The establishment has the normal means of reward, i.e., increased salary, a promotion, greater recognition, etc. However, the agitators—if they are strong enough, numerous enough, and persistent enough—have the capability of rewarding the establishment and the uncommitted by withdrawing the unpleasant phenomenon of agitation. Within their own ranks, the agitators can reward each other by bestowing high office, respect, and other distinctions. (4) The agitators must depend almost completely on referent power and expert power. The members must like other members, and they must be willing to search out and convert more members for their group. The leaders must be able to demonstrate to members and potential members superior knowledge and skill. Unless the leaders of an agitative group are respected and recognized as competent and trustworthy, the actual membership can only decline. The establishment also, of course, has access to referent and expert power. The money spent on public-relations firms, image-makers, consultants, etc., all testify to the recognized need for maintaining these types of power.

The only one of these four generalizations that requires illustration at this point is the last one. An excellent example of the potency of referent power for making converts is Eldridge Cleaver's account of his initial contact with the Black Panther party. Cleaver was already convinced of the need for new kinds of action, so the exercise of expert power was unnecessary. He was attending a meeting of activists planning a commemoration of the death of Malcolm X, when:

> Suddenly the room fell silent. . . . From the tension showing on the faces of the people before me, I thought the cops were invading the meeting, but there was a deep female gleam leaping out of one of the women's eyes that no cop who ever lived could elicit . . . the total admiration of a black woman for a black man. I spun around . . . and saw the most beautiful sight I had ever seen: four black men wearing black berets, powder blue shirts, black leather jackets, black trousers, shiny black shoes—and each with a gun!
>
> Where was my mind at? Blown! . . . Who are these cats? . . . They were so cool and it seemed to me not unconscious of the electrifying effect they were having on everybody in the room.[7]

Cleaver's experience is not unusual. Probably most people who are attracted and held by agitation groups become susceptible by the early use of expert power and are then cued to membership by the attractiveness of members of the agitating group. When the appropriate appeal meets the appropriate susceptibility, membership results.

The establishment, to be successful, must also exercise referent and/or expert power. Thus John F. Kennedy's rise to the presidency and whatever success he enjoyed in it are attributable to his expert, and especially his referent, as well as to his legitimate power. Lyndon B. Johnson declined to run for renomination in 1968, quite possibly because he realized that his referent power had eroded. As we shall show in the next chapter, agitators use the strategy of polarization to attack directly the referent power of the establishment. Similarly, if an establishment loses expert power over its own members, agitation against it is likely to be relatively successful. During the Vietnam war, the Johnson administration became the victim of a "credibility gap" when agitators found it possible to prove discrepancies among "official" statements, other "official" statements, and actual fact. Still, pro-establishment forces continually argued that the administration was in control of the facts and therefore knew best how to devise policy. When an establishment totally loses its referent and expert power, its only chance for survival is in radical adjustment to agitation demands or in violent suppression of dissent.

Sustained agitation almost always has as its principal demand the redistribution of legitimate power. For example, the American labor movement was not primarily a movement for higher pay and better working conditions; rather, it was a movement to secure the legitimate power of collective bargaining and to make legitimate the coercive power of the threatened strike and the strike. The agitation against the war in Vietnam, although it claimed as its goal the end of the war, was also an attempt to curb the exercise of the methods of legitimate power that led to the war. The Chartists in eighteenth-century England opposed a set of tariffs called the Corn Laws, but the main plank in their platform was the legitimate power that would be brought about by a broadened electorate. The various student revolts of the 1960's, although all claimed specific goals, were primarily designed to achieve legitimate power for students by forcing concessions on procedural matters.

Rumor

In agitation and control situations, one mechanism that is frequently used by both sides is rumor. A rumor occurs when information is passed from one individual to another without official verification or denial, or when information is passed from one individual to another in the absence of any trustworthy official source. That is, a rumor can occur either when those in a position to know remain silent or when those in a position to know the truth cannot be relied on to tell it.

It used to be thought that the only necessary conditions to rumors were these: (1) The situation must be ambiguous—more than one interpretation must be plausible. (2) The situation must be relevant to the individual expected to start or sustain the rumor. (3) Trustworthy official interpretations must be absent. Our own research leads us to add another necessary antecedent. (4) The situation must be dramatic, preferably involving conflict.[8]

What happens to a rumor during the course of its life? Three processes have commonly been noted. The first we call *leveling:* Many details get lost as the initial story gets told and retold. The second is *sharpening:* Those details that remain after leveling are exaggerated. The third, and most important, is *assimilation or contrast:* The individual unintentionally distorts the rumor to make it fit more neatly into his own system of beliefs and values. When this distortion is in the direction of what he would most like to believe, it is assimilation; when it is in the direction of what he would least like to believe, it is contrast. As we note in Chapter 3, an establishment must always prepare for the worst. Therefore, when rumors occur in a situation of agitation and control, the establishment distorts by contrast rather than by assimilation. In our analysis of the agitation surrounding the Chicago Democratic Convention of 1968, we discovered that both the agitators and the establishment used contrast—the agitators about the brutality of the Chicago police, the establishment about the number of agitators to expect and their attitudes. Similarly, during the California grape-workers' strike and boycott of the late 1960's, an inaccurate rumor that bartenders were about to boycott Schenley products was probably responsible for that huge corporation's adjustments to the agitators' demands.[9]

Conclusion

In this chapter we have established a frame of reference for the rhetorical analysis of the social phenomena we call agitation and control. Especially important considerations are the structure and function of social organizations, the bases of social power, and the dynamics of rumor transmission. We are now in a position to explain the rhetorical strategies and tactics available to agitators and establishments.

Notes to Chapter 1

1. Kenneth E. Boulding, "Towards a Theory of Protest," *Bulletin of the Atomic Scientists* (1965); reprinted in Walt Anderson (editor), *The Age of Protest* (Pacific Palisades, Calif.: Goodyear Publishing Co., 1969), page vi

2. Hans Toch, *The Social Psychology of Social Movements* (New York: Bobbs-Merrill, 1965), page 3

3. John Robert Howard, "The Flowering of the Hippie Movement," *Annals of the American Academy of Political and Social Science*, CCCLXXXIII (1969), 52

4. Marshall McLuhan, *Understanding Media: The Extensions of Man*, second edition (New York: New American Library, 1964), page 36

5. Daniel Walker, *Rights in Conflict* (New York: Bantam Books, 1968), page 46

6. In Dorwin Cartwright (editor), *Studies in Social Power* (Ann Arbor, Mich.: Institute for Social Research, 1959); reprinted in Dorwin Cartwright and Alvin Zander (editors), *Group Dynamics: Research and Theory*, second edition (Evanston, Ill.: Row, Peterson, 1960), page 607

7. Eldridge Cleaver, "A Letter from Jail," *Ramparts* (June 16, 1968). Reprinted in Anderson, *op. cit.*, page 145

8. John Waite Bowers, *Designing the Communication Experiment* (New York: Random House, 1970), page 78

9. John Gregory Dunne, *Delano: The Story of the California Grape Strike* (New York: Farrar, Straus and Giroux, 1967)

Chapter two

THE RHETORIC OF AGITATION

Assuming that an individual or group advocates a significant social change, and that the establishment opposes this social change, the dissenting group must make choices among the means of persuasion. The more general choices we call *strategies;* the more specific choices governed by these general choices we call *tactics.* In turn, strategies and tactics govern the particular style any rhetorical discourse, thing, or event takes. A moment's reflection will indicate that discourse —written or oral —can be charming or insulting, open or condescending, antagonistic, satiric, etc. Moreover, nondiscursive communication (a police officer making an arrest) can be nonviolent (carrying the offender into a police van) or violent (applying a baton to an offender's vital organs with sufficient force to render him unconscious). We believe, however, that an exposition of the strategies and tactics used by agitators and establishment is more useful than detailing the numerous styles and types of discursive communication.

As we noted in the first chapter, our definition of rhetoric forces us to limit our attention to those aspects of a social movement that are *instrumental* and *symbolic.* Hence we include "revolution" as a strategy of agitation only to give the process an end. Actually, so far as rhetoric is concerned, revolution is consummatory and referential rather than instrumental and symbolic. Similarly, in the chapter on the rhetoric of control, we include "capitulation" as a strategy only to round out the process. Actually, capitulation is not rhetorical. It is consummatory and referential rather than instrumental and symbolic.

The strategies of agitators can be sorted under the following labels: *petition of the establishment; promulgation; solidification; polarization; nonviolent resistance; escalation/confrontation; guerrilla and Gandhi; guerrilla;* and *revolution.* We think that these strategies are more or less cumulative and progressive. That is, we think it unlikely that a strategy lower on the list will occur until all those preceding have occurred. This scaled quality is obviously not perfect, depending on the actual and potential membership of agitation, the power and ideological strength of control, and the rhetorical sophistication of both agitation and control.

The strategy of *petition* includes all the normal discursive means of persuasion. Ordinarily, when social change is deemed desirable, the advocates represent their case to the establishment, marshaling evidence and arguments and indications of the number and kind of people they speak for. Since ordinary rhetorical textbooks devote almost exclusive attention to this strategy, we shall devote very little space to it. Its tactics include those governing selection of motive appeals, selection of target audiences, selection of types and sources of evidence, and selection of linguistic style. By our definition, agitation does not exist when this strategy is used alone. However, its early employment is crucial to an agitational movement, for an establishment, by showing that petition has not occurred, can discredit the agitators as irresponsible firebrands who disdain normal decision-making processes in favor of disturbance and disruption. That is, an agitator is unlikely to be successful unless he can show, before resorting to the more drastic strategies, that he has gone through the normal channels of persuasion. Unless he has done this and has met the control strategy of avoidance or suppression, he is unlikely to win support for or by the more drastic strategies. He must give the establishment an early opportunity to use the control strategies of adjustment or capitulation, no matter how unlikely those responses may be.

Once an agitator has met with avoidance or suppression, however, he is likely to proceed to the strategy of promulgation. This strategy includes all those tactics designed to win social support for the agitator's position. Among these tactics, employed by almost all agitators, are *informational picketing, erection of posters,* and *distribution of handbills and leaflets.* The agitator is also likely to hold a *mass protest meeting.*

The strategy of promulgation as well as all succeeding strategies also includes a tactic that deserves a few paragraphs of its own: *exploitation of the mass media*. One of the main purposes of promulgation, and of all the succeeding strategies, is to win public acceptance of the agitators' ideology, their system of values and beliefs, and policies. This purpose obviously cannot be fulfilled unless they can get exposition of that ideology in a form understandable to the public. The promulgation tactics listed in the preceding paragraph are likely to reach only a few people. The mass media reach many. Obviously, agitators reach more people with less effort if they can get their message carried by the media.

The agitators would like the media to carry their message fully and favorably, but certain economic and political facts of life militate against their success.

They are unlikely to achieve full exposition of their ideology because of the nature of news in the minds of those who control the media. In general, ideologies are not considered newsworthy. The media like to report events, especially unusual events and those involving conflict. In the minds of editors, ideologies make dull reading. If no real conflict is available to report, journalists are likely to select for coverage words that seem to imply conflict, ignoring other ideological elements. This kind of selectivity is well illustrated in *The Autobiography of Malcolm X*:

> But I don't care what points I made in the interviews, it practically never got printed the way I said it. I was learning under fire how the press, when it wants to, can twist, and slant. If I had said "Mary had a little lamb," what probably would have appeared was "Malcolm X Lampoons Mary."[1]

And even later, when Malcolm X stopped stereotyping white people as "devils":

> They called me "a teacher, a fomentor of violence." I would say point blank, "That is a lie. I'm not for wanton violence, I'm for justice. I feel that if white people were attacked by Negroes—if the forces of law prove unable, or inadequate, or reluctant to protect those whites from those Negroes—then those white people would protect and defend themselves from those Negroes, using arms if necessary. And I feel that when the law fails to protect Negroes from whites' attack, then those Negroes should use arms, if necessary, to defend themselves."
> "Malcolm X Advocates Armed Negroes!"[2]

Malcolm X complains that "White reporters kept wanting me linked with the word 'violence.'"[3] Probably it was nothing personal. Reporters report conflict and violence at the expense of other things. In general, the media ignore complicated ideologies.

If agitators have a problem obtaining full coverage from the media, they have an even greater problem obtaining favorable coverage. The reason is not difficult to infer. The principal media in the United States are businesses, profit-making organizations. They are factories. They take raw materials—events and reports of events—and manufacture them into news, which they sell. An important mediator in the process of manufacture is the advertiser, whose dollars sponsor the processes of printing and distributing the finished product.

To succeed, the media must please these groups: (1) those on whom they depend as sources of news; (2) those on whom they depend as sponsors; and (3) those on whom they depend as consumers. Much of their news comes from the establishment, government at all levels, including the enforcement branches, the police, and the military. This establishment is unlikely to be happy with favorable treatments of attacks upon itself by agitators. The second group, the sponsors or advertisers, are notoriously conservative, especially in economic matters. This group probably would withdraw support from any mass communication medium that seemed to advocate (by favorable treatment of an agitation ideology) a new or altered system. Finally, the media depend on their consumers. Most of the consumers are conditioned to accept the dominant value system of the culture, the value system of the establishment. Attacks on that value system make them uncomfortable, and they are likely to begin ignoring the medium that continually carries such attacks.

The system is stacked against agitators who would like to have their message carried fully and favorably by the media. The problem is especially severe for an agitating group that deviates from the establishment laterally as well as vertically, for such a group questions the system's very foundations.

How then can an agitating group exploit the media? As Chapters 4, 5, and 6 will show, two tactics of promulgation are possible. First, to make favorable treatment more likely at least from some media, the agitators are likely to seek *legitimizers*, individuals within the establishment who endorse some parts of the agitators' ideology. Newsworthy individuals like Dr. Benjamin Spock, Senator Eugene McCarthy, and Senator William Fulbright could command the media to some extent during the agitation against the war in Vietnam. This kind of endorsement from individuals the media cannot afford to ignore partially counteracts the built-in bias of the media against agitation ideologies.

Second, in their attempt to get their message across, agitation groups are likely to *stage events that they know to be newsworthy*, events that are unusual or that involve conflict. In their coverage of these events, the media must furnish some rationale, and the rationale may at least partially express the agitators' ideology. As Chapter 4 will show, the agitation itself may sometimes be naturally related to the ideology, so that when the media cover conflict they also expose the agitating message. Sometimes, too, an agitator can exploit his presence at other events to achieve media coverage. On the morning of the day that Apollo 11 began its journey toward the moon, one person who was present at the event, and who was interviewed by CBS for his reactions, was the Rev. Ralph Abernathy. He devoted only a few words to the moon flight, and many words to the plight of poor people in the United States. Similarly, agitators are often called to appear before establishment groups such as congressional committees and disciplinary boards. The media cover the doings of such control groups as a matter of habit, and an agitator can sometimes use his testimony to secure media coverage of his ideology.

The strategy of *solidification* occurs primarily within the agitating group rather than beyond it. Some of its tactics also serve promulgating and polarizing functions, but they are mainly solidifying. By solidification, we mean the rhetorical processes by which an agitating group produces or reinforces the cohesiveness of its members, thereby increasing their responsiveness to group wishes. We include as tactics under solidification a number of symbolic categories that we think are essentially reinforcing rather than persuasive in their relationship to ideology and group membership. The tactics in the strategy include *plays, songs, slogans, expressive and esoteric symbols*, and *in-group publications*.

The agitation play is an interesting form that is now being subjected to scholarly study.[4] It is also a form which is now assuming a dominant place in American theatrical practice. The Living Theater, as well as the many guerilla theater troupes, including the San Francisco Mime Troupe, are essentially agitation theaters.

Usually, an agitation play is a simple dramatization of the grievances of the agitating group. It shows a conflict between agitation and control, coloring the agitators all good and the establishment all evil. Often it includes solidarity words, words in the jargon of the agitating group, such as "scab" and "goon" in a labor play. Sometimes the circumstances of the agitation permit even stronger identification with the audience, as in the case of the guerrilla theater performing for Mexican-American laborers during the California grape strike of the late 1960's, which presented its play both in English and in Spanish.

The plays appeal only to those who are already convinced of the agitators' ideology or who are, because of their grievances, extremely susceptible to the ideology. They take for granted their audiences' familiarity with the situations, conflicts, and resolutions enacted. Often they end unresolved, and exhort the audience to produce a resolution by calling them to action: STRIKE! or MARCH. The best-known such play is a labor play, *Waiting for Lefty*, by Clifford Odets, which was frequently produced during the labor agitation of the mid-1930's. The play is a series of episodes, each episode dramatizing a type of labor conflict and featuring strongly stereotyped agitation and control characters. At the end, the audience has vicariously and actually participated to the extent that an appeal to strike immediately is not unrealistic.

Agitation songs are more varied in content and form than agitation plays, but they share some of the same characteristics. Again, their main function is to assure success through unity in the face of a strong but morally inferior opponent. A large group of such songs have verses simply describing conflict and a chorus emphasizing unity or cohesiveness. Often such songs are lifted from one agitation movement, given new words, and shifted to another. Labor songs seem to dominate later agitation movements. In order to encourage participation, such songs very frequently use the tunes of old popular favorites. "There Once Was a Union Maid" is sung to the tune of "Red Wing." Similarly, "Solidarity Forever" and many derivatives are sung to the tune of the "Battle Hymn of the Republic."

Stephen A. Kaye notes eight characteristics of the language of social-action songs, a category that overlaps considerably with agitation songs.[5] These characteristics are self-explanatory, and they describe not only the language but also the logic of the songs. Kaye sees the songs as marked by "simplicity, redundance, jargon, sentimentality (exaggeration, glorification, fantasy), stereotyping, emotionality, baseness (crudity, viciousness), and humor." Kaye goes on to analyze the argument of the songs and finds it formally deficient, as might be expected of material that serves mainly the function of solidification.

A few songs, more by their melodies and tempos than their words, elicit a feeling almost of reverence toward the cause of protest. Such a song is "We Shall Overcome," the official anthem of the civil-rights move-

ment in its nonviolent manifestation of the 1950's and 1960's. Another—
less solemn but more common in a variety of agitations—is the old hymn,
"We Shall Not Be Moved," a tune amenable to new first lines:

> Harry Bridges is our leader,
> We shall not be moved.
> Harry Bridges is our leader,
> We shall not be moved.
> Just like a tree planted by the water,
> We shall not be moved.

Instead of "Harry Bridges is our leader," agitators might supply "Black
and white together" or any other four- to eight-syllable line.

Songs are not strictly limited, of course, to a solidifying function. Sometimes they also polarize, and we shall say more about them when we
consider the strategy of polarization. Occasionally, they are used strictly
for practical purposes. During the demonstrations at San Francisco State
College, for example, a minstrel preceded the agitators across a busy inter-
section, playing a stringed instrument and singing repeatedly the line,
"Get outa the way."

Another method of solidification is the slogan. Slogans are often
imperative statements, shouted, such as "Stop Dow now," and "Pigs off
campus," and "Power to the people." Sometimes they are single words
or short phrases with the imperative mood strongly implied as in "Black
power" and "Brown power." In complex and prolonged agitations, they
are likely to take the form of a cheer with a cheerleader. At San Francisco
State, for example, a leader would often shout "On strike!" His followers
would answer in chorus, "Shut it down!" As is apparent from these examples, slogans often serve to polarize as well as to solidify, and we shall
consider them under polarization also. One especially potent example
is the now-familiar "Hey, hey, LBJ, how many kids did you kill today?"
This slogan is reminiscent of the old football and basketball yell, "Hey,
hey, whaddaya say, get that ball and fight!"

Agitators often invent expressive and esoteric symbols to accompany
songs, plays, and slogans. These symbols are among the most interesting
of agitative artifacts. Sometimes they are explained with a complicated
mythology, and sometimes they become accepted simply because they are
appropriately powerful or appropriately ambiguous or appropriately well
designed.

The symbol of the peace generation of the 1950's and subsequently was the sign of the anti-Vietnam war agitators. Various explanations are available for this symbol. Simply looking at it, one sees the circle, which is the old religious sign of eternity and of unity; one sees the inverted cross (St. Peter died on one); and one sees three branches from a single stem (the number three has special significance in several religions). One also sees that the design is a simple one, easily reproducible in posters, cartoons, sculptures, and medallions. Possibly, this is enough explanation for the symbol. It has a certain richness of ambiguity. Still, the question of its origin remains. One story has it that the design was scratched into the dust next to a child killed by the Hiroshima atomic bomb. Another theory is that it represents a cancellation sign, a downward slash through an atom-bomb cloud. Others assert that its origin is in Norse runes or in semaphore signals.

The thunderbird was the symbol of the National Farm Workers in their long agitation against the establishment of California grape growers. The black bird against a bright red ground seems to demand attention. Its lines are somewhat reminiscent of ancient Aztec architecture, and this hint of the past is most appropriate, since the grape workers are almost exclusively of Mexican origin. Other than this design feature, we have been able to discover no natural connection between the thunderbird and the National Farm Workers Association. Apparently, members of the Association, or possibly its leader Cesar Chavez, saw the symbol, liked it and adopted it.

Some agitational groups choose their symbols because those symbols have natural relationships to the things they stand for. When Huey

Newton and Bobby Seale sought a name for their militant black party, they found a natural connection with the black panther, a sleek and dignified animal that allegedly does not attack except in self-defense, but then attacks ferociously. The organization became the Black Panther party. Another symbol of the Black Panthers, and one that has generalized its reference so that it now stands for black power (and sometimes brown power and sometimes people power) is the upraised black fist. The fist, like so many tactics that are primarily solidifying, also serves a polarizing function, of course.

The three symbols just described illustrate well the broad range of types adopted by various agitation groups. Some symbols are highly esoteric and ambiguous, like the peace symbol. Such a symbol has broad appeal, for the symbol-user can interpret it in a way that will fit his own value system. The symbol is like a highly abstract word in that it can stand for a variety of referents, any one of which may have special appeal for a given individual. The thunderbird of the United Farm Workers Association is a colorful symbol. It is a more natural, less arbitrary, one than the peace symbol, but no direct connection between it and grape workers is apparent. Still, it is not totally arbitrary, for, as we have mentioned, the shape is reminiscent of Aztec architecture and mythology, and hence is particularly appropriate for an organization comprising almost exclusively members of Mexican citizenship or descent. Finally, the upraised black fist of the Black Panthers and associated organizations is highly natural. It is a nonverbal use of the rhetorical trope synechdoche, a part of something standing for the whole. While it retains some ambiguity (the meaning of "black power" is not a matter of clear consensus), it probably appeals to people holding much narrower ranges of values than does, for example, the peace symbol.

The role of symbols in solidification is probably a highly significant one. The wearing or display of such symbols readily identifies one member of an agitating group for all others. Hence the symbol is a nonverbal, sometimes dramatic, way of saying to those who hold a particular agitating position, "You have my support." Apparently, the establishment appreciates this potency. When two black athletes from the United States raised black-gloved fists during the playing of the Star Spangled Banner at an awards ceremony at the Olympic Games in Mexico City in 1968, an enraged establishment quickly caused them to leave the city. Yet all they had done was to exhibit one symbol, the raised fist, that could have been interpreted either as supporting or competing with another symbol, the Star Spangled Banner.

Some solidifying symbols are kinetic, requiring movement by the symbol-user. A rhythmic, arm-in-arm swaying accompanies the singing of "We Shall Overcome." Eldridge Cleaver describes another kinetic symbol and its effect:

> [The Muslim double handshake] is so popular that one sometimes grows weary of shaking hands. If a Muslim leaves a group for a minute to go get a drink of water, he is not unlikely to shake hands all around before he leaves and again when he returns. But no one complains and the convention is respected as a gesture of unity, brotherly love, and solidarity—so meaningful in a situation where Muslims are persecuted and denied recognition and the right to function as a legitimate religion.[7]

Finally, a method of solidification is the in-group newspaper with its accompanying other in-group printed material. Such publications often have titles that are themselves esoteric symbols. The *Berkeley Barb* has a title that is more or less a natural symbol for an agitating organ. An agitating newspaper at prestigious Grinnell College (one issue of which was seized by law-enforcement agencies) is called the *Pterodactyl*, apparently borrowing the predatory nature of the prehistoric bird. *Ramparts* has an agitating nature, as do the *New Left Review* and *World Revolution*. *Challenge* is a militant title for an agitating publication. Some underground organs, of course, have more prosaic titles, such as the *Spectator* of Michigan.

The contents of agitating newspapers and magazines are likely to stress in-group symbols, stories, and biases. In 1968–69, a syndicate was circulating to leftist newspapers a series of articles on provisioning for and defending against sieges from law-enforcement agencies ("pigs," in the jargon of the group). Probably only a few readers of such publications would ever put into practice the instructions carried in that series. Still, the articles served a solidifying function, stressing for all readers the need for vigilance and devotion to the cause even to the extent of undergoing gassing, beating, and partial starvation.

Of course, in-group newspapers also serve the functions of promulgation (especially in giving credence to rumors) and polarization. Such publications as *Liberation, Ramparts, New York Free Press, Village Voice,* and *Seed* clearly played a leading role in polarizing the city of Chicago in such a way that it would vigorously try to suppress dissent at the Democratic National Convention of 1968.

Almost every agitation movement makes deliberate attempts, once it has attracted a substantial following, to employ the strategy of *polarization*. This strategy assumes that any individual who has not committed himself in one way or another to the agitation is supportive of the establishment. To some extent, this assumption is probably a valid one. Agitators attempt to produce change. The burden of proof is upon them to demonstrate that change is desirable. An individual who has not committed himself to the proposed change can be assumed to be content with the status quo, the establishment way. Since the agitators need a high proportion of explicitly sympathetic individuals, any uncommitted one is not neutral, but is actually counted in the establishment column. The strategy of polarization encompasses tactics designed to move him out of that column and into the agitation ranks, to force a conscious choice between agitation and control.

The two main tactics under polarization are the exploitation of *flag issues* and *flag individuals*. These are issues that and individuals who, for one reason or another, are especially susceptible to the charges made against the establishment by the agitator's ideology. Sometimes, instead of an individual, agitators choose to use a group or organization.

A number of complicated issues were involved in the agitation against the Vietnam war in the late 1960's. These issues involved matters of long-term national policies and priorities and matters of the distribution of legitimate power both nationally and internationally.

But in their demonstrations and in much of their verbalization against the war, the agitators chose to concentrate on one issue: Is it right for the United States to kill Vietnamese civilians, including women and children, with napalm? This was their flag issue.

This issue implied that the agitators would direct most of their energy at certain individuals and groups. Thus, when Dow Chemical Company, a manufacturer of napalm, would send recruiting representatives to a campus, they were likely to be met by a demonstration including the projection of pictures showing napalmed children and the burning of dolls as well as picketing and either orderly or disruptive attempts to keep prospective employees from being interviewed for positions with the company. Marine recruiters were likely to encounter similar treatment, as were ROTC units on the campuses. Other targets were draft boards and virtually all military personnel.

Especially vulnerable as flag individuals were those the public perceived as having most to do with forming and perpetuating American foreign policy. They comprised President Lyndon Baines Johnson, Secretary of State Dean Rusk, Secretary of Defense Robert McNamara, and later Vice President Hubert Humphrey.

Although the demonstrations must have been especially painful to the target groups and individuals, the agitators were not particularly intent on causing pain. They were intent on polarizing individuals uncommitted to their cause. They hoped to accomplish this by forcing such a strong negative reaction to the emotionally charged flag issue that condemnation of flag individuals and groups would follow. Once such condemnation had occurred, recruitment to the more complex and general ideology would be relatively easy. A choice would be forced; neutrality would be most difficult.

Such attempts at polarization occur in almost every agitation. Martin Luther King wrote:

> Shallow understanding from people of good will is more frustrating than absolute misunderstanding from people of ill will. Lukewarm acceptance is much more bewildering than outright rejection.[8]

Because agitators must win converts, must confront the establishment with committed people, those who sympathize with them but do not act with them are worse than useless. Action is the criterion of membership in an agitating group. Inactive members are counted as being with the establishment.

Another polarizing tactic is the *invention of derogatory jargon* for establishment groups. The symbols may or may not have some natural connection to the referents. To a labor union member, the person hired to replace him during a strike is a "scab." An exploiting factory is a "sweat shop." To a member of the International Workers of the World (Wobblies), the Salvation Army was the "starvation army." The labor song "Union Maid" refers to police and other management sympathizers as "goons and ginks and company finks" as well as to a "company stool." In the civil-rights movement, reference is often made to pro-establishment Negroes or uncommitted Negroes as "Uncle Toms" or just "Toms," and the epithet has even generalized into a verb, as in the line of a song, "You're either for the Freedom Ride or you 'tom' for Ross Barnett [former Governor of Mississippi]." Malcolm X, who was extremely aware of the potency of symbols, considered the word "Negro" over-generalized and derogatory, and he liked to refer to non-Muslim Afro-Americans as "so-called Negroes." To many contemporary agitators, all policemen are "pigs." Many members of the New University Conference refer to the establishment in any context as "management," linking it to free-enterprise management in a class struggle with labor. Thus, NUC refers to university presidents and boards of trustees and deans as "management" rather than the more conventional "administration." Finally, agitators may even use the titles of programs as cues to derogatory names. When the agitation against the anti-ballistic missile system (ABM) was hot, one agitator published a poster labeling the system America's Biggest Mistake.

The most interesting strategy of agitation is *nonviolent resistance*. This was the strategy of Gandhi and Martin Luther King, Jr. It has also been employed by other groups in America, including some abolitionists, some pacifists, some suffragettes, and some trade unionists.[9]

Basically, the strategy of nonviolence places agitators in a position in which they are violating laws they consider to be unjust, destructive of human dignity. (Sometimes customs rather than laws are violated.) Usu-

America's
Biggest
Mistake

ally the agitators simply do the things they would be permitted to do if the laws they are violating were changed. Arthur I. Waskow calls such activities "creative disorder."[10] They include sit-ins, school boycotts, rent strikes, and the like.

If the establishment accedes to the demands of the agitators, the disorder ends. If the establishment resists, it must do so by physical suppression. That is, no way of ending the agitation is open to the establishment except the physical removal of the agitators.

In a society in which the laws are extremely unjust, this suppression is likely to be violent. The nonviolent resister predicts violence. His theory is that if this violent suppression becomes known, and if he does not react to violence with violence, the larger community will release pressures on that section in which the unjust laws exist, pressures to cease the violence and to change the laws. If the larger community reacts as the nonviolent resister predicts, then the agitation has succeeded without destroying the trust upon which the existence of community depends. In a sense, the agitator has had victory without war.

In 1958, Dr. King outlined some aspects of the nonviolent philosophy:

First, it must be emphasized that nonviolent resistance is not a method for cowards; it does resist. If one uses this method because he is afraid or merely because he lacks the instruments of violence, he is not truly nonviolent. . . . This is ultimately the way of the strong man. . . . The phrase "passive resistance" often gives the false impression that this is a sort of "do-nothing method" in which the resister quietly and passively accepts evil. But nothing is further from the truth. For while the nonviolent resister is passive in the sense that he is not physically aggressive toward his opponent, his mind and emotions are always active, constantly seeking to persuade his opponent that he is wrong. The method is passive physically, but strongly active spiritually. It is not passive nonresistance to evil, it is active nonviolent resistance to evil.[11]

In other words, all the energy of the nonviolent resister is directed at the policy he is violating. None of his energy is used up in attempting the destruction of the perpetrators and preservers of that policy.

Dr. King's second aspect of nonviolence is that it does not seek to defeat or humiliate the opponent, but to win his friendship and understanding.

The nonviolent resister must often express his protest through non-cooperation or boycotts, but he realizes that these are not ends themselves; they

are merely means to awaken a sense of moral shame in the opponent. . . .
The aftermath of nonviolence is the creation of the beloved community, while
the aftermath of violence is tragic bitterness.[12]

The third aspect emphasizes the impersonal nature of the resistance,
or rather, the extra-personal nature of it; the attack is directed against
forces of evil rather than against persons who happen to be doing the evil.

It is evil that the nonviolent resister seeks to defeat, not the persons victimized
by evil. . . . I like to say to the people in Montgomery: "The tension in this
city is not between white people and Negro people. The tension is, at bottom,
between justice and injustice, between the forces of light and the forces of
darkness. And if there is a victory, it will be a victory not merely for fifty
thousand Negroes, but a victory for justice and the forces of light. We are out to
defeat injustice and not white persons who may be unjust."[13]

Dr. King's fourth aspect is the key one for nonviolent resisters:

[Nonviolent resistance requires] a willingness to accept suffering without
retaliation, to accept blows from the opponent without striking back. . . . The
nonviolent resister is willing to accept violence if necessary, but never to
inflict it. He does not seek to dodge jail. . . . Suffering, the nonviolent resister
realizes, has tremendous educational and transforming possibilities. "Things
of fundamental importance to people are not secured by reason alone, but
have to be purchased with their suffering," said Gandhi.[14]

The fifth aspect of the philosophy concerns the internal state of the
resister:

[Nonviolent resistance] avoids not only external physical violence but also
internal violence of spirit. The nonviolent resister not only refuses to shoot
his opponent but he also refuses to hate him. . . . Along the way of life, someone must have sense enough and morality enough to cut off the chain of
hate. This can only be done by projecting the ethic of love to the center of
our lives.[15]

The sixth aspect is an optimistic conviction about the nature of life:

[Nonviolent resistance] is based on the conviction that the universe is on the
side of justice. Consequently, the believer in nonviolence has deep faith in the
future. This faith is another reason why the nonviolent resister can accept
suffering without retaliation. For he knows that in his struggle for justice
he has cosmic companionship.[16]

Dr. King's aspects of nonviolent resistance are a mixture of pragmatic
directions and philosophical generalizations. The strategy, insofar as we

are concerned with it, consists of actively resisting laws or customs in such a way that the establishment must either succumb or remove the resisters. Assuming that the establishment decides to remove the resisters, they must not react aggressively no matter what provocation occurs. To use the strategy in a given agitation, not all the agitators (or, even, not any of them) need accept Dr. King's convictions about the nature of the universe or the existence of cosmic love. Dr. King himself admitted that "there are devout believers in nonviolence who find it difficult to believe in a personal God."[17] Whether such belief exists or not, nonviolent resistance has been shown to be a potent agitation strategy.

Nonviolent resistance differs from the other agitation strategies we have considered and will consider because, in the polarization stage, it does not attempt to derogate the individuals in the establishment. That is, a nonviolent resister directs all his attention at flag issues, none at flag personnel.

Often, the term "civil disobedience" is used in conjunction with non-violence. Civil disobedience occurs when an agitator deliberately breaks a statute that he considers to be unjust and destructive. Nonviolent resistance is not always civilly disobedient, but it often is. When it is not, the agitators are violating custom rather than law. We see no need to distinguish between civilly disobedient resistance and other kinds, except to say that changing a law requires a longer formal process than does changing a custom.

The questions might be raised: (1) Is nonviolent resistance consummatory rather than instrumental? (2) Is it referential rather than symbolic?

Clearly, in almost all cases, nonviolent resistance to customs and laws is instrumental rather than consummatory. A sit-in at a lunch counter or a boycott of a bus system does not accomplish the integration of the lunch counter or the bus system. It is a means to that end. The outcome may not be the integration of the lunch counter or the bus system at all. It may be, if the establishment is sufficiently resistant, the closing of the business, or it may be, if the agitation movement is weak, the successful suppression of the agitators. Whatever the outcome, the nonviolent resistance is instrumental rather than consummatory. Most often, it involves civil disobedience, which implies that the agitators' goal is the repeal of a law or the enactment of new laws, ends that the resistance by itself obviously cannot accomplish.

Is nonviolent resistance symbolic? Almost always, it is. The agitators use the presence (or, sometimes, the absence) of their bodies as symbols of their extremely strong convictions about laws and customs. We have already made the distinction between arbitrary symbols (such as the relationship between a word and its referent) and more natural symbols (such as the relationship between a picture of an upraised fist and its referent). The dominant symbol in nonviolent resistance, the body of the agitator, is on the natural end of the continuum. Still, it is not meaningful in itself; it must be interpreted. Nonviolent resistance involves one of the cooler symbol systems in the rhetoric of agitation. The agitators typically do not have the opportunity to make their message verbally explicit through the media. The target audience must ask themselves: What would cause people to put their physical selves in jeopardy in such a manner and without threatening retaliation for physical harm? The audience must then supply its own answers to the question. According to the theory of the agitators, this supplying of the answers should result in the involvement of the audience in the movement. Our study of the agitation in Birmingham, Alabama (Chapter 6), shows how accurate the theory can be, given an extremely strong agitation group wholly committed to nonviolence and an extremely resistant, suppressive establishment.

Nonviolent resistance requires, probably more than any other agitation strategy, the tactic of *persistence*. A nonviolent resister poses no actual threat of destruction to the establishment. The establishment need not fear a fight, so it cannot act as though a war exists. On the other hand, neither can the establishment ignore the nonviolent agitator. His presence is a nuisance, preventing the establishment from making money or doing business as usual. The typical response of the establishment is to remove the agitators. Once that is done, the establishment has suppressed the agitation, unless the removed group is replaced by another group in such a manner that the nuisance is continued. (Some nonviolent resisters furnish a new kind of nuisance in jail by staging hunger strikes, prayer meetings, songfests, and the like.) The agitators must have the manpower to continue the nuisance persistently until social change occurs. St. Luke furnished a good illustration of the theory:

> And he said to them, "Which of you shall have a friend and shall go to him in the middle of the night and say to him 'Friend, lend me three loaves, for a friend of mine has just come to me from a journey, and I have nothing to set before him'; and he from within should answer and say, 'Do not disturb me; the door is now shut, and my children and I are in bed; I cannot get up and give to thee.'

"I say to you, although he will not get up and give to him because he is his friend, yet because of his persistence he will get up and give him all he needs. And I say to you, ask, and it shall be given to you; seek, and you shall find; knock, and it shall be opened to you. For everyone who asks receives; and he who seeks finds; and to him who knocks it shall be opened. But if one of you asks his father for a loaf, will he hand him a stone? or for a fish, will he for a fish hand him a serpent? or if he asks for an egg, will he hand him a scorpion?"[18]

Another special requirement of the nonviolent resister, since he is a nuisance to the establishment, is that he be most careful to have exhausted the avenues of petition and verbal rhetoric before he begins his physical resistance to the law or custom. Again, Martin Luther King, Jr., in his defense of the Birmingham agitation, was foresighted enough to see that this exhaustion of the verbal means of persuasion would be necessary if the movement were to influence others. He writes:

In . . . negotiating sessions certain promises were made by the merchants—such as the promise to remove the humiliating racial signs from the stores. On the basis of these promises Rev. Shuttlesworth and the leaders of the Alabama Christian Movement for Human Rights agreed to call a moratorium on any type of demonstrations. As the weeks and months unfolded we realized that we were the victims of a broken promise. The signs remained. As in so many experiences of the past we were confronted with blasted hopes, and the dark shadow of a deep disappointment settled upon us. So we had no alternative except that of preparing for direct action, whereby we would present our very bodies as a means of laying our case before the conscience of the local and national community.[19]

Later in the same document, Dr. King wrote, "History is the long and tragic story of the fact that privileged groups seldom give up their privileges voluntarily."[20]

The strategy of nonviolent resistance subsumes two principal tactics. The first of these is that in which the *physical presence* of the agitators may be presumed to produce what Dr. King called "creative tension."[21] The sit-down strike, devised by American trade unionists in the early twentieth century, is one example of the use of this tactic. Other examples are lunch counter sit-ins, public pool and beach swim-ins, university teach-ins, and the like. The second uses the *physical and/or economic absence* of the agitators to create tension leading to negotiation and adjustment. The Montgomery, Alabama, bus boycott of the middle 1950's is probably the most noteworthy example. Conventional labor strikes also use this tactic.

A strategy that has only recently begun to be exploited by agitators is *escalation/confrontation*. This strategy has its base in social psychology, and the major principle underlying the strategy is this: When the establishment becomes sufficiently apprehensive, it will overprepare for agitation. This overpreparation will result in such confusion among establishment groups that security forces of the establishment will turn on themselves and on non-agitators. Hence the establishment will be made to look foolish, and its inadequacies will be demonstrated.

The strategy has been used in a number of urban riots and disturbances. Robert Gover, the novelist, satirizes the workings of the establishment mind in his book, *J C Saves*. The narrator of these passages is J. C. Holland, a city's public information director:

> They'd been rioting in city after city across the nation, but not here. "Don't Let It Happen Here"—this was a motto both the city and the county were combined on. We'd enlarged both our police forces, given the firemen riot training, spent thousands for special riot equipment, and we'd alerted the National Guard. We'd done everything we could think of to prevent it, you see, so when it came we were beautifully prepared. . . .
>
> Skipping on for the moment, to the final body count, we lost only one. A fireman in a tragic incident. He somehow got in the way of a speeding ambulance which was evacuating some policemen who'd been wounded by ricocheting bullets.
>
> Later it was determined that our tactics proved too much for those would-be looters. Our firemen stayed a jump ahead of the arsonists and most of the loss suffered by local merchants was due to water. Our nip-it-in-the-bud strategy worked beautifully.[22]

Gover's description is of the outcome when the strategy of escalation/confrontation is successful.

The strategy consists of a series of tactics, each of which is designed to escalate the tension in the establishment until finally establishment representatives resort to violent suppression in a confrontation with the agitators.

The first tactic is what we call the tactic of *contrast*. Its objective is to ensure that the establishment will expect the participation of large numbers of agitators, whether this expectation has any objective reality or not. The agitators realize that the establishment must prepare for the worst conceivable outcome. This tactic involves the use of rumor and the underground press to inform the establishment that, in terms of numbers, the worst conceivable outcome might be very bad indeed.

The second tactic in the escalation, still preceding the actual agitation, is *threatened disruption*. Building on the establishment's specter of large numbers of agitators, this tactic again uses rumors and the underground press to increase establishment tension with alleged information about the attitudes and objectives of the agitators. These threats prepare the establishment for deliberate disregard of laws and the destruction of establishment property if not personal security.

Once the agitation is actually begun, the agitators employ a *nonverbal offensive*. They are likely to dress in strange ways. They display posters and carry signs scornful of establishment values. They sing songs and may make gestures offensive to the establishment.

They simultaneously or subsequently use *verbal obscene deprecation*. In Chicago in 1968, two of the most frequent agitative chants were "Fuck LBJ" and "Fuck Daley." Policemen were addressed in terms that the establishment considered taboo and insulting. At this stage also, the agitators may employ the tactic of *non-negotiable demands*.

The verbal obscenity might be followed by *nonverbal obscenity*. In Chicago, agitators threw feces and urine at police. These objects were symbolically aggressive. (They were not actually aggressive, for feces and urine are not weapons designed to cause much physical harm.) They also spit at the police, and some agitators disrobed in front of the establishment representatives.

These agitative tactics are likely to lead to the violent confrontation desired by the agitators. However, if they do not, the agitators can resort to *token violence*. This involves actual, but minor, attacks on representatives of the establishment by a few of the agitators. The strategy assumes that the establishment will respond to such attacks with counterattacks far out of proportion to the original provocation. Confrontation will have occurred. The establishment will have exposed itself in what the agitators think of as its true colors.

The last three agitative strategies are only partly rhetorical; the final one is not rhetorical at all, and we included it only for the sake of completing the system.

The strategy of *Gandhi and guerrilla* confronts the establishment with a large group of agitators committed to the strategy of nonviolent resistance and another group committed to physical destruction of the establishment. The first group is rhetorical, for their behavior is instrumental and symbolic. The second group is mainly nonrhetorical, for their behavior, though instrumental, is actually, not symbolically, aggressive. The strategy assumes that the activities of each group will contribute to the achievement of common goals.

The strategy of *guerrilla* is symbolic only to the extent that physical, underground attacks on an unpopular establishment, if successful, will polarize other disaffected members of society to the extent that they will join in the attacks. For the agitators, the attacks are real, not symbolic. However, they may serve as demonstrative symbols to others.

The strategy of *revolution*, of course, is not symbolic. It is war.

Conclusion

In this chapter, we have briefly described the principal strategies employed by agitators. *Petition* and *promulgation* are strictly verbal. If a movement confines itself to them, agitation has not occurred. *Solidification* and *polarization* reinforce members of the movement and induct those who are sympathetic but uncommitted. *Nonviolent resistance* results in "creative tension," which may lead to the resolution of grievances by negotiation. *Escalation/confrontation* is designed to goad the establishment into disproportionate violence, prompting the larger society to institute reforms. *Gandhi and guerrilla, guerrilla,* and *revolution* are increasingly nonrhetorical, involving actual physical attacks on the establishment in a win-lose frame of reference, rather than from a compromise and reform point of view. The next chapter proposes a rhetorical theory of control strategies.

Notes to Chapter 2

1. *The Autobiography of Malcolm X* (New York: Grove Press, 1964), page 243
2. *Ibid.*, page 366
3. *Ibid.*, page 367
4. Weldon Durham, "Theater of Agitation and Control," University of Iowa Kinescope, 1970
5. Stephen A. Kaye, "The Rhetoric of Song: Singing Persuasion in Social-Action Movements," unpublished doctoral dissertation, University of Oregon, 1966
6. *Ibid.*, page 74
7. Eldridge Cleaver, *Soul on Ice* (New York: Dell, 1968), page 52
8. Martin Luther King, Jr., *Letter from Birmingham City Jail* (Philadelphia, Pa.: American Friends Service Committee, 1963), pages 3–14. Reprinted in

Staughton Lynd (editor), *Nonviolence in America: A Documentary History* (Indianapolis, Ind.: Bobbs-Merrill, 1966), page 470

9. For amplification, see Lynd (editor), *op. cit.*

10. Arthur I. Waskow, *From Race Riot to Sit-In* (Garden City, N.Y.: Doubleday, 1966), page 225

11. Martin Luther King, Jr., "Pilgrimage to Nonviolence," in *Stride Toward Freedom* (New York/Harper and Row, 1958), pages 90–107; reprinted in Lynd (editor), *op. cit.*, page 391

12. *Ibid.*

13. *Ibid.*, pages 391–392

14. *Ibid.*, page 392

15. *Ibid.*

16. *Ibid.*, page 395

17. *Ibid.*

18. Luke, 11:5–12

19. King, *Letter from Birmingham City Jail*, in Staughton Lynd (editor), *op. cit.*, pages 463–464

20. *Ibid.*, page 466

21. *Ibid.*, page 465

22. Robert Gover, *J C Saves* (New York: Pocket Books, 1969), pages 7–10

Chapter three

THE RHETORIC OF CONTROL

Writing in 1513, Machiavelli suggested in *The Prince* that establishments can be rank-ordered in terms of power:

> A prince, therefore, should have no care or thought but for war, and for the regulations and training it requires, and should apply himself exclusively to this as his peculiar province; for war is the sole art looked for in one who rules, and is of such efficacy that it not merely maintains those who are born princes, but often enables men to rise to that eminence from a private station (Chapter xiv).

If we broaden Machiavelli's conception of a "prince" to encompass the decision-makers within a given establishment, and if we understand by "war" an establishment's response to external assault on its structure, goals, or power, then we can begin to appreciate the role of power in control groups.

Decision-makers, much like the leaders of an agitation group, maintain their position in the power hierarchy in two general ways. Within an establishment they must repeatedly give evidence of their "superiority." By this we mean that the decision-makers must show that their ability to manage, guide, direct, and enhance the group is greater than that of other members in the group. For example, if a company commander is to evoke loyalty, compliance, and respect from his enlisted men, he must demonstrate his superior physical, psychological, and/or intellectual strength. That rhetoric, as it is customarily interpreted, plays an important role in maintaining decision-makers in their position of power is almost axiomatic. Our concern in this chapter, however, is with the way that decision-makers respond to external challenges. Specifically, we shall focus on the rationales which govern the discursive and nondiscursive communication used by decision-makers to cope with agitation from without.

One principle governs the rhetorical stance taken by any establishment: *Decision-makers must assume that the worst will happen in a given instance of agitation.* The corollary to this principle is equally important: *Decision-makers must be prepared to repel any overt attack on the establishment.* Alan Barth, editorial writer for the *Washington Post,* recently underscored these principles of control:

> Establishments, generally speaking, are better equipped than student revolutionaries and guerrilla fighters with brass knuckles, tear gas, Mace, shotguns and the like; and they are far less squeamish about employing them. . . . In the end, victory goes to the most ruthless.[1]

One need only consult the national defense budgets of major nations to appreciate the cost of being prepared to repel challenge. In a somewhat lighter vein, however, the principle of assuming the worst sometimes generates incongruous events. During one campus demonstration a flat piece of cardboard painted to represent a gigantic firecracker was tossed toward several policemen. The painted cardboard had an ignited fuse taped on one edge. A senior officer immediately ordered the crowd to clear the area; two sergeants stomped out the wilted fuse; another was sent for a fire extinguisher. While the crowd chuckled at these elaborate precautions, a much-chastened "bomb-maker" was arrested. In a later interview the officer explained that he assumed a real bomb might be attached to the cardboard.

An establishment's public image is enhanced when it can demonstrate to its membership that preparations have been sufficient to thwart external attack. Also, when an establishment has confronted external challenge in the past, it can use those confrontations as a justifying reason for accelerating its preparations for the worst eventuality. After experiencing many student protests, riots, and demonstrations in 1968, college administrators stiffened and enlarged their security forces to be ready for future disruptions. An Associated Press survey in the fall of 1969 revealed that the Universities of Maryland and Texas increased their campus police forces, and Temple University formed its own 125-man security staff. The University of North Carolina adopted regulations which read in part:

> Any student or faculty member—including full time or part time instructors—who wilfully by use of violence, force, coercion, threat, intimidation or fear obstructs, disrupts or attempts to obstruct or disrupt the normal operations or functions of any of the component institutions of the univerisity, or who incites others to do so, shall be subject to suspension, expulsion, discharge or dismissal from the university.[2]

And in a similar manner Cornell now has rules banning not only attempts to obstruct university operations, but also "firearms, language likely to incite the use of physical force, and persistent noise."

One writer summed up the preparedness principle in this way:

> The administration of control is suspicious. It projects a dangerous future and guards against it. It also refuses the risk of inadequate coverage by enlarging the controlled population to include all who might be active in any capacity. Control may or may not be administered with a heavy hand, but it is always a generalization applied to specific instances.[3]

Projecting an image of strength determines, in large part, the referent power necessary for maintaining the institution.

We maintain that when a regulatory agency is confronted with proposals requiring change in the establishment's structure, policy, ideology, or power, it can adopt one of four rhetorical strategies: *avoidance, suppression, adjustment,* or *capitulation.* Depending on the perceived threat to the institution and the power of the group espousing the differing ideology, an establishment can decide to use its resources to avoid, suppress, adjust, or capitulate to the changes sought by the agitative force.

If an establishment elects a strategy of *avoidance,* a number of tactics are available to deal with the ideology and its proponents.

The decision-makers themselves or their representatives may choose, for example, a tactic of *counterpersuasion.* Entering into a discussion with the leaders of an agitative movement in an attempt to convince the agitators that they are wrong serves a number of functions for the establishment. If counterpersuasion is successful, the threat to the system is minimized. If unsuccessful, the establishment has still gained time and avoided any significant revision of establishment ideology and structure.

As a tactic, counterpersuasion is the most common and often successful maneuver available to an establishment. To the child's pouting and wailing symbolic behavior, intended to make his parents attend the county fair, a counterpersuading father might suggest attending a drive-in movie, a less-costly goal substitution. A senator often has formulary responses to use in countering petitions he receives in the mail. And just as an agitator dares not bypass the petition phase of his campaign, an establishment dares not refuse to engage in counterpersuasion. Ubiquitous public relations firms, complaints departments, "information" offices, white papers, grievance and bargaining committees, etc., attest to the frequency with which establishments engage in counterpersuasion. If an agitator elects to move beyond the petition-counterpersuasion phase, decision-makers within the institution can inform their membership that the agitators would not listen to reason, and thus the decision-makers gain implicit approval for other control strategies and tactics.

From the counterpersuasion tactic, decision-makers can shift to a strategy of adjustment more easily than from any of the other control tactics we shall discuss. An establishment would be inconsistent if it imprisoned an agitator and then openly declared that his proposals had been accepted.

If an organization is large enough, it can use a tactic of *evasion*. Synonyms are "buck-passing" and "the runaround." A sizable bureaucracy can effectively avoid consideration of many challenges by routing the leaders of the agitation movement through the labyrinth of receptionists, outside secretaries, inside secretaries, private secretary, low-level administrator, receptionist, outside secretary, etc.

To illustrate both the existence and possible complexity of evasion, we cite an actual case which occurred recently at a midwestern university. A group of students tried to start a collective housing experiment. Many professors supported the project, and several teachers wished to use the experiment for research purposes. The university's regulations specifically prohibit students under 21 from living in unapproved housing; yet the experiment necessitated students under 21 living in unapproved housing.

The odyssey began when the students met with the dean of academic affairs to secure a place on the agenda of a student-faculty committee. The dean of academic affairs referred them to the dean of student affairs, who promised moral support and sent the group back to the dean of academic affairs, who notified them that the agenda of the student-faculty committee was filled. Undaunted, the group petitioned each committee member the evening before the committee was to meet. At the meeting the next day, the age-suspension resolution passed. But the resolution needed the approval of the president who, having resigned some months earlier, requested: (1) that the president-elect make the decision, and (2) that the resolution be returned to the dean of academic affairs, who, when contacted by the students, claimed that he had not seen the resolution.[4]

A more serious instance of evasion occurred in 1968 at Tokyo University. In January the students demonstrated to abolish the intern system, by which professors use intern students to do research without pay. One critic described the ensuing events in this way:

> The medical students went to see Prof. Toyokawa, the Chairman of the Medical Department, to talk about abolishing this intern system. They couldn't see him. In fact, Prof. Toyokawa prides himself on the fact that he never sees students. . . . Seventeen students were punished for being active in the demonstration and for causing disorder at the school. . . . The university authorities punished by dismissal or forced holidays instead of talking with them. The authorities never talk to them. . . . This trick worked very well up to this time. . . . But this time, the story is a little different, because these seventeen students included a student, Mr. Tsubura, who wasn't at school when the demonstration occurred; he was in Kyushu, some distance from Tokyo. The students asked Prof. Toyokawa . . . to withdraw the punishment because of the inaccurate facts. He said he didn't make any mistake and the President, Okochi, supported him. . . .
>
> In April 1968, the students had a sit-in on the campus. By this time, the trouble was not only in the Medical Department but had spread to the whole school. . . .
>
> On June 16, the authorities requested the Tokyo riot task force, which takes care of disorders, to get the students off the campus. . . . Never before had the task force invaded the campus. . . . The students . . . took the attitude of force against force.[5]

The *Walker Report* of the 1968 Chicago agitation clearly indicates that Mayor Daley used the tactic of evasion. Permits to use Lincoln Park after the curfew hours were requested by the National Mobilization Committee as early as June 16 and were finally denied by Chicago authorities on August 5. The convention began August 25.

Evasion can be a tactic of high risk for an establishment. If an agitative movement is sufficiently powerful, the leaders may simply go to the President's house, or Washington, or the Pentagon, or a state legislature. An establishment, then, by evading a confrontation with a dissident ideology, runs the risk that the dissidents will appeal to a higher, more powerful establishment. When the Delano grape strikers were unable to plead their case with the Schenley and DiGiorgio Companies, they marched 300 miles to the governor's mansion in Sacramento.

As we have indicated, evasion is a tactic best suited to a large establishment. Less powerful and smaller establishments may use a tactic of *postponement*. By deferring any binding decision and by taking the demands of an agitative group "under advisement," an establishment can frequently avoid unwanted change. Creating fact-finding and *ad hoc* committees, actively scheduling subsequent board meetings, conferences, and commissions, and urging further dialog may all serve as effective impediments to the external challenge of the agitators. At least two factors favor an establishment's using the tactic of postponement: (1) The agitators may become impatient and reckless. If they break a civil law, they can be jailed. (2) The agitators may be patiently persistent and wait, which allows an establishment to defer indefinitely.

Another tactic of avoidance is that of *secrecy with a rationale*. An existing power structure can hear the demands of agitators and openly decline any response by appealing to a higher principle. When an establishment is sufficiently confident of the cohesion and loyalty of its membership, considerable time and effort can be saved by using this tactic. However, the principle invoked must, indeed, be higher in the members' hierarchy of values than the accepted practice of responding to petitions. The actual manufacturing cost of an American automobile, for example, is never divulged. The reason: "Competitors would undercut our price and destroy us." Before the Truth in Lending Law of 1968, interest rates were frequently and sometimes intentionally obscured for prospective borrowers. The rationale: "Other lending agencies might loan money at lower rates." One can find enough cases of news management for reasons of national security to exemplify this tactic. And "national security" was among the rationales offered to the public in the recent Green Beret case. When the litigation required that CIA officials be called to testify in the trial, Army Secretary Stanley Resor issued the following statement.

> I have been advised today that the Central Intelligence Agency, though not directly involved in the alleged incident, has determined that in the interest of national security it will not make available any of its personnel as witnesses in connection with the pending trials in Vietnam of Army personnel assigned to the 5th Special Forces group.
>
> It is my judgment that under these circumstances the defendants cannot receive a fair trial. Accordingly, I have directed today that all charges be

dismissed immediately. The men will be assigned to duties outside of Vietnam.

While it is not possible to proceed with the trials, I want to make it clear that the acts which were charged, but not proven, represent a fundamental violation of Army regulations, orders and principles.

The Army will not and cannot condone unlawful acts of the kind alleged. Except in the rare case where considerations of national security and the right to a fair trial cannot be reconciled, proceedings under the Uniform Code of Military Justice must take their normal course.

It would be unjust to assess the culpability of any individual involved in this matter without affording him an opportunity to present his defense in a full and fair trial. Under our system of jurisprudence, every man accused of wrongdoing is presumed to be innocent until he is proven guilty. The determination of guilt may. be made only by a court which has access to all information with respect to the alleged offense.[6]

If an establishment issues a rationale unacceptable to its own membership (we suspect any rationale for secrecy given to agitators is, by definition, unacceptable to them), serious consequences result. The credibility gap created during the Johnson administration is an instance attributable to selecting an unacceptable rationale for official secrecy.

An institutional authority also has at its disposal an avoidance tactic which we shall call *denial of means*. To effectively promulgate their ideas and demands, an agitative group must have certain physical means to do so. Paper, ink, duplicating equipment, cameras, recording devices, sound equipment, meeting halls, parks or demonstration areas are essential tools for agitation.

One group of agitators in the archdiocese of Washington decided to use St. Matthew's Cathedral as a public forum for their accusations and demands. To deny the protesters the means of making their demands public, the cathedral organist pumped deafening music into the cathedral when the agitators assembled, rendering speech-making impossible.[7]

By ripping the wires from a sound truck, President S. I. Hayakawa on one occasion denied the San Francisco State agitators the physical means for being heard. Mayor Daley denied the Yippies the use of Soldier Field; President Hesburgh of Notre Dame once denied agitators the use of Notre Dame property. An institution, however, must exercise great caution in denying an agitative group the means for promulgating their ideas. Granted, the board of directors at Dow Chemical would *not* normally be expected to provide duplicating paper and sound equipment to an anti-napalm organization. But a city government that allows its parks to be used for celebrating the Fourth of July may well be expected by the public to let the parks be used by apparently peaceful demonstrators.

An establishment dares not violate constitutional rights of free speech and free assembly; consequently, *justifying reasons must be issued simultaneously with a denial of physical means.* At the Democratic Convention in 1968, speakers who argued against the Johnson administration frequently found their microphones abruptly turned off. To our knowledge, no justifying reasons were announced; no one even bothered to claim technical difficulties.

When, in 1960, the House Un-American Activities Committee held allegedly open hearings in San Francisco, part of the ensuing demonstrations on Black Friday were attributed to HUAC's ticket policy. To attend the hearings, one needed a ticket, and to get a ticket, one had to belong to the American Legion, the DAR, or some similar organization. Denying the means of protest—in this case, a seat in the hearing room—was an outright violation of the principles of fair play; it became public knowledge and probably caused even more citizens to oppose the House Committee. Again, to our knowledge, no justifying reasons for the ticket policy were announced.

As a tactic of avoidance, however, denying believers in an opposing ideology the physical means of making their grievances public can weaken, if not eliminate, an agitative movement. Senator Eugene McCarthy's supporters in many cases were denied attendance at the Democratic Convention in 1968; Martin Luther was denied his pulpit for a period of time; and for many years, in parts of the South, Negroes were not allowed to attend political caucuses. On a superficial level, denial of means may seem to be a low-order tactic. It is not always so. When agitators use strategies of nonviolent resistance to call attention to their grievances, establishments have a ready-made rationale for creating new policies bordering on suppression. In the wake of the student protests, confrontations, and guerrilla activities in 1968–69, many state legislatures passed resolutions to deny future agitators the means of advancing their causes. Marquis Childs indicated the scope of these resolutions when he wrote:

> West Virginia is farthest out, with six bills passed this year that virtually wipe out all constitutional guarantees of the right of assembly and privacy. Police or mayors "shall be held guiltless" if anyone is killed or wounded in the attempt to put down an uprising, even if the victim is a spectator.

In other states pending measures or those already passed go nearly as far. In Wisconsin the effort is to keep out out-of-state students with cries that the minorities—Negroes and Jews—are responsible for all the trouble.[8]

Ironic though it may be, agitators, by using strategies of nonviolent resistance, may trigger the creation of a more repressive and restrictive system. Yet establishments often do not respond—except by avoidance— to the petitions of agitators until protest goes beyond the conventional verbal methods of communication.

A second rhetorical strategy an establishment can adopt in responding to external challenge is *suppression*. Our hypothesis is that institutions usually do not resort to suppression until most or all of the avoidance tactics have proved futile. Suppression demands not only an understanding of the opposing ideology but a firm resolve and commitment on the part of the decision-makers to stop the spread of the ideology by thwarting the goals and personnel of the agitative movement. Whereas most of the avoidance tactics focus on changing or retarding the issues underlying the agitation, most of the suppression tactics seem to focus on weakening or removing the movement's spokesmen.

Usually the first tactic of suppression is *harassment* of the agitator's leaders. Although this maneuver is ostensibly directed at the power figures in an agitation movement, harassment actually seems better designed to weaken and dilute the solidarity of the agitating group's membership. Just as any establishment needs its leaders to guide and direct the institution, so an agitative group needs leaders to maintain a cohesive, unified membership. When agitative-group leaders encounter suppressive harassment, two consequences inevitably occur: (1) The key personnel of the agitative movement have less time to devote to their cause and their sympathizers, and (2) the members of the agitative group view the harassment as an example of what may happen to them if they persevere in their beliefs and activities.

Harassment encompasses a broad spectrum of establishment activities. When decision-makers threaten to resign unless the agitation ceases, for example, a certain kind of moral force is deployed. On the other side of the spectrum, however, different types of force are deployed. FBI raids on the Chicago Black Panther headquarters provide a vivid example of planned harassment against avowed revolutionaries. During the first six months of 1969, Black Panthers were involved in more than 60 criminal prosecutions and posted $300,000 in bail bonds. On June 4, eight Panthers were arrested at their headquarters for harboring a fugitive from Federal authorities (who was not in Chicago); weapons, literature, lists of donors, office equipment, etc., were also confiscated. Five days later, eleven Panthers were arrested, again near Panther headquarters, and charged with possession of marijuana. On the following morning, simultaneous raids were made on Panther buildings in New York, New Haven, Oakland, Salt Lake City, Des Moines, Denver, and Indianapolis. That afternoon in Chicago, sixteen Panthers were indicted on conspiracy charges. Trying to put the raids in perspective, Kermit Coleman, ghetto project director of the American Civil Liberties Union, said:

> As long as you talk about black capitalism, you don't go to jail. But when you come out of a revolutionary bag that doesn't encompass the present political and economic structure, that's when all the powers of repression are brought to bear.[9]

Returning for a moment to the Machiavellian metaphor of decision-makers as "princes," we can extend the image by considering their "allies." Establishments, when they are harassing an agitative group, frequently receive unsought assistance from other sources. When Malcolm X became identified as a key figure in the Black Muslims, his house was attacked with rocks, shotguns, and eventually fire bombs. Eldridge Cleaver and Bobby Seale, recognized spokesmen for the Black Panthers, were accorded similar treatment. Madalyn Murray, leader of the movement to ban prayers in public schools, was temporarily forced to leave the United States after repeated attacks on her property and threats on her life. And the early history of the labor movement in the United States provides abundant examples of active, deliberate harassment from para-establishment groups. Vigilante organizations usually emerge to combat large-scale agitation. In the aftermath of campus protest in 1968–69, Louis Byers formed The National Youth Alliance, which was openly dedicated to "ridding our schools of pinkos, Marxists, and black and white gangsters." Byers explained how his organization would respond to campus protest:

> Let's say the following happens—some communistic SDS members (Students for a Democratic Society) take over a student union building somewhere. Well, then, right away our people will meet to react.
>
> At first we will do everything possible, peaceably, to get the rowdies evicted. We will apply pressure on the administration, the local community, and the police—to try to get a general uprising.

But if nothing happens this way, then we'll have to resort to final means. We'll organize enough people and enough force to physically enter the building—and toss the militants out ourselves.[10]

Of course, harassment of an agitative group, if it is inopportune, overly harsh, and adequately publicized, can cause backlash. In a sense, however, harassment functions as a testing maneuver. If the agitation ceases after its leaders or members have been harassed, the regulatory agency need not employ other suppressive tactics and the agitative ideology no longer poses a threat to the institution. If agitation is sufficiently solidified, as it was for the Southern Christian Leadership Conference in 1963, then each act of harassment (bombing, burning, jailing, etc.) not only increases the solidarity of the agitative forces, but also tends to weaken the referent power of the decision-makers within their establishment.

Perhaps the most obvious suppressive tactic is an overt *denial of the agitators' demands*. In 1967 many college administrators were presented with ultimatums to end military recruitment on campus. Usually the demands were denied. One group at Berkeley demanded that Eldridge Cleaver be allowed to teach a seminar in their Black Studies Program. Chancellor Heynes said no. The Third World Coalition Movement at San Francisco State College demanded that President Hayakawa retain a certain faculty member. The demand was denied.

As a tactic, however, saying no is a gamble for an institution. If an establishment has legitimate power, there is some risk that the law may eventually be interpreted in favor of the agitators. For example, in a Des Moines, Iowa, high school recently, John and Mary Beth Tinker, sophomores at the school, demanded that they be allowed to wear black armbands to protest the war in Vietnam. They were suspended. The case reached the Supreme Court, and wearing armbands was found to be a legal exercise of free speech. Hence the gamble: The very legitimacy invoked to deny the demand may be changed by a higher authority.

Moreover, the tactic of denying demands may precipitate and generate increased power in the ranks of the agitative group. If the denial is interpreted as an injustice by some members of the establishment, internal dissension may result and the establishment's decision may be rescinded. A case in point is that of Jerry Sies, a frequent activist at the University of Iowa, who demanded the right to examine city records on substandard apartment housing. On Monday he was denied the right to do so by a city official. Members of the city council and the local judiciary joined his cause, and the city records were made available on the following day. For an institution to deny demands, therefore, is a feasible tactic only when the legitimate and referent bases of power are sufficiently and clearly supportive of the stance taken by its decision-makers.

However, when the legitimate power group and the referent power groups within an establishment differ in ideology, denial of demands causes more damage within the establishment than damage to the agitative group. At San Francisco State College, the Board of Trustees (legitimate and reward power) held beliefs opposed to those of the faculty (referent power). By denying the demands of the militant teachers and students, President Smith appeased the Board, enraged the faculty, and was forced to resign.

Two other suppressive tactics are available to some establishments: *banishment* and *purgation*. Although the word banishment may seem unnecessarily archaic, we know of no other term that encompasses such instances as these:

1. Excommunication
2. Expulsion
3. Academic suspension
4. Compelling someone to leave an area under the laws of illegal assembly
5. Encouraging or forcing someone to leave the physical boundaries of a country
6. Confining someone in jail

Since relatively few members of an agitative movement usually carry its grievances and ideology to the decision-makers of an establishment, the tactic of banishment can terminate a movement by removing its leaders and spokesmen.

In recent months many cases of banishment can be cited. As a group of students at the University of Denver began to stage a sit-in, the president, Maurice B. Mitchell, expelled them. The action enabled the city police to come in and take them off the campus. The sit-in ended before the movement gathered momentum, and his action was upheld by the courts.[11] President Hesburgh of Notre Dame allows 20 minutes for anyone who "substitutes force for rational persuasion, be it violent or nonviolent." After 20 minutes demonstrators are automatically expelled, or, to use our term, banished. *The Chronicle of Higher Education* noted: "In California, the state university's Board of Regents ordered that whenever the governor declares a state of emergency, administrators must put on interim suspension anyone charged with disruptions, banning him from the campus."[12]

J. Edgar Hoover said in his report on FBI activities during fiscal 1969 that campus disorders resulted in more than 4000 arrests. In addition, the roll call of academic banishment indicates the utility of this tactic: San Francisco State College, 1 expelled, 22 suspended; Harvard, 16 expelled; Wisconsin State at Oshkosh, 90 expelled; Kansas, 33 suspended; Chicago, 43 expelled, 81 suspended; Berkeley, 15 expelled, 35 suspended.[13]

For two years college undergraduates who had 2S (educational) draft deferments and who participated in antiwar or antidraft activities faced banishment by losing their draft deferments. Selective Service Director Lewis B. Hershey reasoned that these deferments were issued in the national interest, and that anyone trying to hamper the draft or public policy could not be acting in that interest. The United States Court of Appeals later ruled that draft boards had no right to reclassify registrants because of antiwar activities, but, at the same time, upheld the draft system's right to reclassify those who violate delinquency regulations.

Instances of banishment are abundant. Castro exports his counterrevolutionaries at the rate of 1000 per week. The Berrigan brothers, convicted of destroying Selective Service records in Catonsville, Maryland, now reside at a medium-security correctional institution in Danbury, Connecticut. Martin Luther King, Jr., was jailed more times than St. Paul. At the San Francisco Presidio stockade in 1968, 27 GI's protested unsanitary conditions and the killing of a prisoner. While attempting to read their grievances, they were charged with mutiny, a capital offense. They were convicted. Many Black Panther leaders now live outside the U.S. Eldridge Cleaver, black author and a Panther leader, has been in exile in Algeria. Byron Booth, Panther deputy minister of defense, and Earl Farrow, deputy minister of information, probably took refuge in Cuba. H. Rap Brown faces a felony charge the moment he re-enters New York state. And some five to ten thousand young men who now live in Canada may return to the United States only by paying the tariff of five years in jail.

Of all the tactics an establishment can use, banishment is probably the most effective. Few movements can survive without leadership, and banishment not only removes the leaders but also serves as an exemplary deterrent to the members of an agitative group. It is dangerous to control, however, when the banishing establishment violates its own regulations, thereby eroding its legitimate power.

By the tactic of purgation, we mean, simply and literally, killing the leaders and members of the agitative movement. Only a political establishment with a powerful military force can use this tactic. In addition, such a political establishment must be sufficiently confident of its strength to be willing to risk a possible war with allies of the agitators. For example, the Boxer Rebellion in 1900 was crushed by an allied force of 20,000 troops; the Hungarian Freedom Fighters were mauled by Russian tanks in 1956. In both cases, no one helped the agitators.

A third rhetorical strategy is *adjustment*. Institutions can adapt, modify, or alter their structures, their goals, and their personnel as a response to an external ideological challenge. The adjustment must never be perceived by those who support and maintain the decision-makers as a concession or partial surrender, nor should an agitative force claim that an adjustment is, in fact, a concession. Whenever an establishment adjusts to a new ideology, more than semantics is at stake. Weakness is not a virtue, especially weakness in the decision-makers of a regulatory, control agency. The dynamics seem to work in this manner: Agitators make a demand, those in control decide to adjust. If agitators declare a victory and use language connoting concession *and* if the members of the establishment *believe* that their decision-makers have yielded when confronted with an external challenge, then the strategy of adjustment is no longer available to an institution. Decision-makers may be just, merciful, liberal, progressive, open-minded, etc., but they may *never* be weak.

In much the same way that the tactics of suppression can be either nonviolent or violent, the tactics of adjustment can be apparent or real. For example, the tactic of *changing the name of the regulatory agency* after a confrontation with an agitative group is seldom a real adjustment in an establishment's structure, personnel, or ideology. The House Un-American Activities Committee is now known as The House Committee on Internal Security. The negative-income-tax proposal is rapidly becoming known as a special "family security system." And on one Big Ten campus, after serving as the focal point for demonstrations against Dow Chemical and Marine recruiters, the Business and Industrial Placement Office was renamed the Office of Career Counseling.

Changing an institution's name, while it rarely satisfies any agitative ideology, does serve to refocus and clarify the institution to those within the establishment. Specifically, the tactic tends to solidify those members of the establishment who are removed from the decision-makers, yet share the essential values of the institution.

When agitation is addressed to a flag person, a second tactic of adjustment—*sacrificing personnel*—is usually available to the establishment. Instances come easily to mind. Lyndon Johnson sacrificed himself as an adjustment following the antiwar demonstrations of 1967–68. Grayson Kirk of Columbia, Nathan Pusey of Harvard, Morris Abram of Brandeis, Clark Kerr of the University of California, and Robert Smith of San Francisco State probably were sacrificed as adjustments to campus disorders. This tactic carries some risks for the decision-makers: The channels of communication within an institution suffer from the temporary vacancy, time must be allocated to finding a replacement, and the legitimate power of an establishment becomes vulnerable. To counter this last hazard, most establishments use the tactic of sacrificing personnel to elicit sympathy for the victim and to arouse the moral indignation of the members of the establishment against the agitators who made the tragedy necessary. Agitative polarization is most easily accomplished if a flag person can be located to personify the grievances of the agitative group. When the flag person is removed from the establishment, the agitative group suddenly finds itself without a cause, and its energies must be redirected toward maintaining its own membership. Because of the underlying similarity of values of those within an establishment, the replacement for the sacrificed flag person rarely is an individual whom the agitators themselves would have selected.

A third tactic of adjustment involves *accepting some of the means of agitation*. Not getting arrested is no way to make headlines or network news. Widespread attention must be focused on the issues and ideology of agitative groups, and one method of attracting attention is using creative disorder. Yet, if the creative disorder goes unnoticed, agitation may be effectively thwarted. For example, one group of Aid to Dependent Children mothers, demanding higher benefits based on the cost of living, staged a camp-in on the state-house grounds of a midwestern city. No arrests were made; there was virtually no television coverage; and the camp-in ended after one night. In a three-inch news story, the governor later said, "We didn't really provide a camping service for these people. They wanted to express themselves. They did no one any harm."[14] One form of creative disorder used by antiwar demonstrators has consisted of reading lists of servicemen killed in Vietnam. For a time people were arrested, on various charges, for assembling to read these lists. Such readings, without arrests, later were commonplace and ineffective events.

Accepting some of the means of agitation works much like a draw play in football. Some of the opposition are purposefully allowed through the line, only to discover that where they had been is where the football went. Extending the analogy, an establishment can actually provoke agitators to engage in increasingly more serious infractions of law or custom. If a sit-in goes unnoticed, agitators, to gain an audience, must risk escalating the creative disorder. Disturbing the peace is a relatively insignificant misdemeanor, and by judiciously waiting for agitators to increase the intensity of their symbolic behavior, a shrewd establishment can later impose more severe penalties, up to and including banishment. Also, accepting some of the means of agitation can be extremely useful to an institution in post-confrontation rhetoric, to demonstrate the institution's strength to its members. It implies a nice element of institutional broad-mindedness which, when contrasted with the guerrilla activity of agitators, enables the decision-makers to justify the later harshness of their suppressive measures.

An institution that elects to adjust to external challenge has at least two other tactics at its disposal. It can *incorporate some of the personnel* of the agitative movement, or it can *incorporate parts of the dissident ideology*.

Black faculty members and administrators now command high salaries in Northern universities. Students now serve on many college committees. In California, several grape growers and supply firms created the Agricultural Workers Freedom to Work Association, hired three Mexican-Americans as officers of the association, and attempted to drum up public opposition to the table-grape boycott by claiming to speak for the farm workers. Perhaps the most obvious instance of incorporating personnel was reported in *Time* as follows.

> College trustees were once interested primarily in saving money and having winning football teams. Though the average age of trustees still hovers well beyond the half-century mark, a few schools have begun to foster a youthful image.
>
> The nation's first under-30 university trustees, most of them recent graduates [some of them earlier militants], have been appointed this year at Maine, Lehigh, Princeton and Vanderbilt. The eight state universities in Kentucky have begun to admit student leaders as ex-officio trustees. In Vermont, Wyoming, and Washington, legislatures are weighing proposals to name youthful members to state university governing boards.[15]

Incorporating the personnel of an agitative movement may be expensive and, in some instances, deceitful. As a tactic, however, incorporating dissident personnel tends to modify both the establishment and the agitative movement. Activists can see some visible effect of their efforts; the establishment can use the new personnel as lackeys or mediators or possibly as decision-making colleagues.

Much the same is true with respect to the final adjustment tactic of incorporating parts of the agitators' ideology. The incorporation may range from tokenism to a substantial merger. A university, for example, may consent to buy some books by black authors for its library, or institute a black-studies program, or refuse to do business with firms that discriminate in their hiring practices. The executive committee of the National Council of Churches recognized the National Black Economic Development Conference after James Forman presented his Black Manifesto to the NCC in 1969. Since hindsight is always 20–20, one might say that the city of Chicago should have granted rally permits to the National Mobilization Committee and, possibly, free balloons and Mayor Daley Love Beads to the Yippies.

To incorporate the ideology of an agitative movement into the consensus of beliefs of an establishment is delicate business at best. The decision-makers must maintain their necessary image of strength, establishment's membership must not perceive the change as altering in a significant way the values and goals of their institution; and both agitative and control groups may need to effect considerable understanding and compromise before this tactic of adjustment becomes possible. Nonnegotiable demands, by definition, do not admit of realistic adjustment.

The last strategy an institution may adopt is *capitulation* to the challenging ideology. To be totally successful, an agitative movement—its ideas, goals, policies, beliefs, and personnel—must replace those of the target institution. An example is the regime of Fulgencio Batista in Cuba, which capitulated to Fidel Castro's agitative force in 1958.

We know of no instance in which an establishment has surrendered all its decision-making power voluntarily. From this we infer that capitulation is an establishment's last resort. Further, we infer that no established regulatory agency uses this strategy unless total destruction by a superior force is imminent. And since total capitulation is neither instrumental nor symbolic, it is not rhetorical. It is complete defeat.

We have now considered the theory governing the agitative situation and the rhetoric of the social organizations involved. We have neglected to specify the nature of the interaction between agitators and establishments except informally, by way of illustrating the separate theories. We shall reserve a discussion of that interaction for Chapter 7, after we consider cases of agitation and control in Chapters 4, 5, and 6.

Notes to Chapter 3

1. Alan Barth, "Urges Student Activists: Use Brains, Not Weapons," *Des Moines Register*, September 4, 1969, page 6

2. Garven Hudgens, "Crackdown on Protests Foreseen," *The Daily Iowan*, September 10, 1969, page 3

3. Michael E. Brown, "The Condemnation and Persecution of Hippies," *Transaction, VI* (1969), page 33

4. Note: Larry Chandler, "Bureaucrats and Tactics: An Example," *The Daily Iowan*, June 28, 1969, page 2

5. Ikuo Uchida, "Student Riots—Japan Style," *Pacific Speech Quarterly, III* (1969), page 28

6. UPI release printed in *The Cedar Rapids Gazette*, September 29, 1969, page 1

7. *The National Catholic Reporter*, June 18, 1969, page 2

8. Marquis Childs, "Crippling Storm May Hurt All Campuses," *The Cedar Rapids Gazette*, May 9, 1969, page 4

9. Jerry DeMuth, "Chicago Cops Crack Down on Panthers," *National Catholic Reporter*, June 25, 1969, page 1

10. Tom Tiede, "Vigilantes Train to Combat College Militants," *The Cedar Rapids Gazette*, June 25, 1969, page 11

11. Jeffrey Hart, "A Stiffening of Academic Backbone," *National Catholic Reporter*, March 12, 1969 page 8

12. *The Chronicle of Higher Education*, March 10, 1969, page 12

13. Philip W. Semas, "Find Colleges Tougher Than Critics Have Said," *Des Moines Register*, August 24, 1969, pages 1–2

14. *Cedar Rapids Gazette*, July 7, 1969, page 2

15. *Time*, August 29, 1969, page 37

Chapter four

AGITATIVE MOBILIZATION: CHICAGO, AUGUST 1968

The years 1967 and 1968 saw a sharp rise in political activism, including agitation, among America's young. Almost every major college campus had its instances of nonviolent resistance and confrontation prompted by institutional compliance with such national policies as permitted the war in Vietnam. The more general reasons for this youthful activity, which followed a long period of apparent political apathy, are difficult to isolate. Certainly, the stresses accompanying the "triple revolution" in warfare, cybernation, and human rights had something to do with it.[1] Injustices were becoming more visible, and idealistic young people, reared with a rationale of independent thought and social action, were responding to them. *The Walker Report to the National Commission on the Causes and Prevention of Violence,* on which this chapter depends heavily, notes as causes "the civil rights movement, the peace movement, the changing role of universities, the changing emphasis of organized religion, the growth of an affluent middle class, the ubiquity of television, the stresses of urbanization, and the failure of federal, state and city governments to find solutions to social problems fast enough to satisfy aspirations raised by the solutions they *have* found."[2]

Suddenly, young people were noticing arbitrarily oppressive elements in American culture. They had witnessed and participated in the early years of the blacks' agitative struggle for equality. They were being drafted to fight in a war that many thought imperialistic. And the decision-making mechanism—the establishment—seemed determined to ignore their demands.

Background

Here we examine one manifestation of the new activism and institutional response to it: the agitation and control surrounding the convention of the Democratic party in Chicago, August 25–29, 1968. We do this from a rhetorical point of view, seeking a persuasive rationale for the words and the symbolic acts of the agitators and the establishment.

The account concerns itself mainly with the rhetorical behavior of four groups of people, three agitative and one establishment. The agitating groups were the National Mobilization Committee to End the War in Vietnam (hereafter called Mobilization), the Youth International Party (hereafter called Yippies), and the Coalition for an Open Convention (hereafter called Coalition). Mobilization and the Yippies were clearly agitative groups, from the beginning of their planning for the convention to its aftermath. Coalition, a group consisting mainly of young people who supported the candidacy of Eugene McCarthy, had confined its pre-convention activity to petition and conventional political activity. In the convention city itself, however, it became an agitative group, lending moral and sometimes physical support to the acitivies of the other two groups. The establishment was represented by the City of Chicago.

A number of identifiable events, beginning in the spring of 1967, were clearly relevant to the agitation in Chicago. A chronological listing of these events appears as Appedix A to this chapter. Biographical sketches of a few agitative and establishment leaders appear as Appendix B. Most of the information in these appendixes is from the *Walker Report*.

Chicago was tense on the eve of the convention. Telephone, taxi, and transit strikes had affected the city for months. The broadcasting media were dissatisfied because these strikes, as well as some rules instituted by the convention leaders, made live-camera coverage impossible in many parts of the city and many parts of the convention. A number of delegates to the convention were also unhappy with the situation. Some had tried to move the convention out of Chicago, attempts which Chicago's Mayor Richard Daley vigorously rebuffed. The broadcasting media also had indicated that the convention might be moved—to Miami, where they had already established their facilities for coverage during the previously held Republican convention. Many residents of Chicago apparently perceived the agitating groups as being invaders of the city, though the number of agitators who came to Chicago was small (about 10,000) compared with the city's previous estimates. From January 1968 onward, the city itself had prepared for the convention and the anticipated agitation in at least a dozen agencies. Apparently, its plans had assumed that at least 150,000 protesters would be in Chicago.[3]

Ideology of the Establishment

The establishment, of course, accepted the dominant ideology of the nation, or at least what it perceived to be the dominant ideology. In its judgment, the status quo, at least as far as the allocation of political power was concerned, had only minor deficiencies. Decisions should be made by those to whom the American political/economic system had given legitimate power. Once those decisions were made, all other Americans should patriotically support their implementation. Those in the best position to guide the destiny of the nation were those selected as leaders by the system. The judgment of these leaders could be questioned, but only verbally. This ideology had carried the nation triumphantly, in the mind of the establishment, through World War I, the great depression, World War II, and the Korean War.

More specifically, the war in Vietnam was justified as being in the interests of the nation and its dominant ideology of national prestige and power. Economic, social, and political inequities in the United States should be eliminated, but for the moment the war took precedence. National pride demanded that the country continue on the course it had taken.

The convention itself, said the establishment, was operating in the venerable tradition of the American political system. The Democratic party gave each voter an equal voice in the choosing of the candidate. If the methods of the states varied, it was a matter of custom, not malice. The party's system had worked and would continue to work. The candidate of the party would be the people's choice.

Even if inequities did exist, they must not be allowed to manifest themselves in the form of disruption. Law and order must be preserved. America's political system could not operate amid chaos, and those who would cause chaos must be discouraged by any means necessary.

Ideology of the Agitators

The three agitative groups, although they disagreed on the best means to produce change, did agree on certain basic matters of ideology. Mobilization, Yippies, and Coalition were dissatisfied with the same sorts of things.

The three groups agreed that the American economic/political system, as objectified in the Democratic party, was deficient. Specifically, they agreed that the war in Vietnam was unjust and imperialistic and that the government of the United States had misrepresented the nature of the war to its citizens. They further agreed that the system was arbitrarily discriminatory against blacks and certain other groups and that the Democratic party had not done enough to eliminate this discrimination. Finally, they agreed that the government and the party failed to live up to the ideals of democracy, in that certain elements (the professional politicians, the military/industrial complex) held disproportionate decision-making power. If the people knew the truth, the agitators maintained, that power would be repudiated. They pointed out in support of this claim that the candidate who would be nominated by the party had not won or even entered a single primary election.

The ideological differences of the three agitative groups lay in the means they would adopt to correct the situation. The Yippies opted for anarchy. Mobilization leaned toward a system of socialism. Coalition had hopes for the status quo and attached those hopes to a single candidate, Eugene McCarthy.

Petition and Avoidance

Two of the agitation groups, Mobilization and Yippies, began planning for Chicago in late 1967. They followed conventional channels of petition in their attempts to ensure that they would have available the means for their protest.

On May 10, 1968, Abbie Hoffman, a New York Yippie leader, was in Chicago to make Yippie plans for the "Festival of Life" with the Chicago group. At that time, the Chicago group decided to dissociate themselves from the New Yorkers, naming themselves the Free City Survival Committee. This committee began negotiating with the city for various kinds of permits early in the summer of 1968.

Throughout the summer, both Mobilization and Yippies attempted to negotiate two kinds of applications. The first kind requested the city to suspend its 11 P.M. curfew for activity in the city parks so that visitors to Chicago could sleep there. The second kind was for parade permits. The agitators wanted authorization for parades to the Chicago Amphitheater, where the convention was to be held, and for parades around the downtown hotels, where the delegates were to be housed. Mobilization also applied for a permit to use Soldier Field for a rally. In its application, Mobilization estimated that 150,000 people might participate in its parade and rally.

Chicago postponed action on all the permits until August 5. On that date, it refused permission to sleep in the parks and announced that the 11 P.M. curfew on activity in the parks would be enforced. (According to the *Walker Report*, this curfew had been interpreted flexibly on a number of occasions prior to the convention.) The city postponed action on the parade and rally permits until August 21, four days before the convention was to begin. It denied permits to march to the Amphitheater and around the downtown hotels, proposing instead alternative routes, which the agitators found unacceptable. It denied the use of Soldier Field, at first with the rationale that the stadium was needed for a celebration of President Johnson's birthday, later with the explanation that National Guard troops would be quartered there.

Mobilization appealed these decisions in the courts. On August 23, almost on the eve of the convention, Federal Judge William J. Lynch, whom the agitators identified as a law partner of Mayor Daley, denied the appeals.

Finally, on August 27, two days after the convention had begun, the city issued a permit to Mobilization for an afternoon rally the following day in Grant Park.

Nonviolent Resistance and Suppression

Agitators in appreciable numbers began arriving in Chicago simultaneously with the beginning of the convention, August 25. Many of them, of course, had no place to stay. Since most of their acitivities were in the city's parks, they attempted to sleep in the parks in violation of the curfew.

The city responded with suppression. Nightly during the convention, the police cleared the parks at the curfew hour. In addition, the *Walker Report* tells of various attempts to suppress the agitators in other areas, especially the Old Town section of Chicago, which was ideologically most hospitable to protest. The city enforced its laws to the letter: no loose livestock in the city limits, no marches or rallies without permits, no defacing of public property.

The peculiar situation governing the broadcasting media in Chicago made it possible for the city to carry out its suppression at this point with virtually no publicity. Live television cameras were permitted only in the Amphitheater. In addition, the city and police, according to many reports, deliberately interfered with efforts of newsmen to cover the violence. Finally, the unavailability of focused sites for agitational acitivity made any reliable coverage impractical early in the convention.

Escalation/Confrontation and Suppression

What made the Chicago situation unique was the complex series of events, their interpretation, and their consequences that we have labeled escalation/confrontation and suppression. In the account that follows, we are frankly interpreting those events. We attribute intentions, motives, and states of mind to agitators and establishment. It is a long account and sometimes a frightening one.

The general strategy of the agitators

How could the agitators get their message across to the public in a favorable light? One way would be to goad the city of Chicago, America's second city, into actions that could be viewed as a microcosm of all the domestic and foreign oppressions fostered by the American system. If the police responded brutally to an orderly demonstration, or even to minor violations of the law, then the agitators would have made their point. Syllogistically:

Chicago acts as the United States acts.

Chicago acts brutally and oppressively.

Therefore, the United States acts brutally and oppressively.

If the agitators could convince the public that the two premises of this syllogism were true, they would dramatically and rhetorically make their ideological point.

Obviously, the news media would cover the Chicago story in force. Any analyst would realize that the Chicago story embodied two newsworthy elements: the conflict accompanying the agitation and the activities of the convention itself. The conflict itself was one message the agitators wanted to transmit, for such conflict was bound to place the protesters in the role of underdog. (The agitators' chant, "The whole world is watching," during the most violent part of the suppression, makes it clear that they recognized the value of television coverage.) However, the message would also be transmitted by speakers in the convention itself, members of the establishment who disagreed with its dominant ideology, speakers like Paul O'Dwyer of New York and Julian Bond of Georgia. The convention gave the agitators an unusual opportunity to have their message made explicit and fully carried by the media.

The general problem of the agitators, then, was to devise a combination of tactics whose result would be public, direct, and violent suppression by the city. Such a strategy would escalate the intensity of the conflict between agitators and establishment until an exploitable confrontation occurred.

The tactic of contrast

The agitators knew that Mayor Daley and the Chicago police tended to suppress agitation violently. This had been demonstrated by the mayor's statement during the rioting following Martin Luther King's assassination that the police should "shoot to kill arsonists and shoot to maim looters." It had also been demonstrated by the excessive use of police force to break up an April 1968 peace march in Chicago. If given the chance, Chicago could be depended on to perceive events in such a way that it would prepare for grave danger to itself. The agitators could exploit the city's tendency to prepare for the worst conceivable threat.

When the agitators began planning for Chicago, they were already in a strong position as far as promulgation and solidification were concerned. On April 15, 1967, Mobilization, as an umbrella for approximately 150 other organizations, had staged a peaceful protest march of 100,000 people to the United Nations building in New York city. On October 21, 1967, the same organization had sponsored a march of 50,000 on the Pentagon in Washington. About 5000 individuals in this march had provoked some violence.

Prospects for a huge demonstration were enhanced by circumstances during the winter of 1968 when plans were being formed. Lyndon Johnson was in the White House, and seemed virtually assured of renomination by his party. The agitators had already frequently and successfully exploited his potential as a flag individual for their protests against the system. During the fall of 1967 and into the winter and spring of 1968, then, forecasts like the following, from a Mobilization newspaper, were credible:

> We may find that we meet each other again in Chicago ... because the tactical situation will be good. ... If there are 100,000 people on the streets, prepared to do civil disobedience, what should their demands be?[4]

Mobilization's prospects for a massive demonstration in Chicago were augmented by statements from representatives of other groups. Dick Gregory was promising to bring about 100,000 blacks, and Abbie Hoffman and Jerry Rubin estimated the Yippie contingent in the tens of thousands. One guess during this planning period about the number of protesters who would come to Chicago was as high as a million.[5] Since Lyndon Johnson and the war combined to lend credibility to such estimates, Chicago began preparing for at least 150,000 agitators.

From February onward, events combined in such a way that a realistic analyst would have revised his estimates drastically downward. In February 1968, Eugene McCarthy's candidacy for the presidential nomination of his party became a serious threat to the administration. His candidacy brought into the establishment great numbers of young people who had been potential agitators. On March 12, McCarthy's candidacy was impressively reinforced by his unexpected victory over President Johnson's stand-in when the nation's first primary election was held in New Hampshire.

Almost immediately, Senator Robert Kennedy brought thousands of potential agitators into the establishment by announcing his candidacy for the Democratic nomination. In retrospect, Yippie leader Abbie Hoffman recognized the potency of Kennedy as an establishment leader who would be followed by those susceptible to agitation:

> But Bobby there was the real threat. A direct challenge to our theater-in-the-streets, a challenge to the charisma of Yippie. ...
>
> *Come on,* Bobby said, *join the mystery battle against the television machine.* Participation mystique. Theater-in-the-streets. He played it to the hilt. And what was worse, Bobby had the money and power to build the stage. We had to steal ours. It was no contest.
>
> Yippie stock went down quicker than the money we had dumped on the Stock Exchange floor.[6]

The greatest blow to agitation's hopes for numerical impressiveness occurred on March 31, 1968, when Lyndon Johnson announced that he would neither seek nor accept his party's renomination. The most provocative of agitation's flag individuals had abdicated.

In April, Chicago took action that would have the effect of discouraging from coming to Chicago any individuals who wished to avoid violence. We have already mentioned the "shoot to kill arsonists and shoot to maim looters" order and the violent suppression of the April 27 peace march, which drew only about 6500 agitators.

In late April and early June, the agitators' dying plans received two transfusions: Hubert Humphrey announced his candidacy for the nomination, and Robert Kennedy was assassinated in Los Angeles. The transfusions did not produce recovery. Vice President Humphrey, because of his impressive credentials as a liberal, was a much less satisfactory flag individual than Lyndon Johnson had been, although in his pre-convention statements the Vice President pledged to carry on the policies of the Johnson administration in Vietnam. The Kennedy followers who might have joined an agitation movement if no other recourse were available had assimilated—with some success—establishment procedures, and most found it possible to change their allegiance to McCarthy, to Humphrey, or to Senator George McGovern, who declared his candidacy later. Finally, in spite of Dick Gregory's earlier statements, the agitators failed to attract substantial black support.

All but the most earnest agitators were further discouraged by Chicago's failure to grant permits for sleeping in the parks and for orderly demonstrations. Many who might have come in spite of the establishment's intransigence were persuaded to stay away on August 12, 1968, when Senator McCarthy, in view of the violence that by then seemed almost inevitable, requested that his supporters not come to Chicago during the convention. The senator's statement must have been a strong deterrent to those who wanted to voice dissent but who feared violence.

Despite this chain of events, Mobilization and the Yippies continued to claim up to 150,000 potential agitators throughout the summer of 1968. Chicago took this inflated estimate seriously, as establishments are prone to do, and prepared for an invasion of hostile hordes. Chicago has 12,000 policemen. In addition, the Mayor put under the command of the police 11,000 National Guardsmen.[7] These troops, bristling defensively with armor and tanks, were assigned to control the 10,000 agitators Mobilization and the Yippies managed to assemble in their most successful moments. The tactic of contrast had produced the potential for violent suppression.

Threats to disrupt

Mobilization and the Yippies combined their efforts effectively with threats to disrupt the convention. Some of these threats were apparently serious, others obviously put-ons. The city, following our generalization that establishments prepare for the worst, apparently took them all seriously.

The Mobilization threats were frequent and public. The organization had proved itself capable of producing violence during the Pentagon march the preceding October. Some of the early Mobilization statements made explicit the intent of agitation to employ the tactic of Gandhi and guerrilla:

We have to have two hats—nice and violent.[8]

One veteran of the Washington march suggested that volunteers be urged to disobey any curfew, in order to force the police into a mass arrest situation.[9]

I think we can do better than attempting to prevent the Convention from taking place, as some have suggested, by closing down the city on the first day of pre-Convention activity.[10]

We are flexible enough to permit each to act in his own style and we will support all of our associated groups.[11]

Dick Gregory is reported to have notified President Johnson that unless racial conditions were improved in Chicago he would lead demonstrations "which would make it possible for the Democratic party to hold its Convention here only over my dead body."[12] [Gregory's home is in Chicago.]

We'll stop the convention if we have to burn down the hall.[13]

I would like to see us . . . release the real power of our many forces in a new and significant way at the time that Johnson is nominated, turning delegates back into the Amphitheater as they attempt to leave.[14]

Many similar statements are available from more or less official Mobilization spokesmen. Clearly, the threat of disruption was explicitly available to haunt Chicago throughout the summer. The city's plans to prevent disruption, begun in January, became more and more involved.

Possibly to protect themselves later, or possibly because they changed their minds about the efficacy of disruption after President Johnson withdrew, at least two Mobilization leaders, Rennie Davis and Tom Hayden, issued statements disclaiming any plans to disrupt. Davis said, reporting on a July 1968 meeting of Mobilization:

And then we had a long discussion . . . and it was quite clear at the end of that meeting that there was no opposition to my interpretation of their slogans [some members were wearing "Stop the Convention" buttons] — interpreting it to mean the end of this kind of politics in America without a literal interpretation to disrupt the convention.[15]

Hayden more consistently than other Mobilization leaders issued statements disclaiming any intent to disrupt. However, he understood clearly that, whether intended or not, disruption might result from the agitation in view of the city's preparation for the presence of 150,000 protesters:

Consider the dilemmas facing those administering the regressive apparatus. . . . They cannot distinguish "straight" radicals from newspapermen or observers from delegates to the convention. They cannot distinguish rumors about demonstrations from the real thing. . . . There is a point beyond which the security system turns into its opposite, eclipsing the democratic image and threatening the security of the convention itself. The threat of disorder, like all fantasies in the establishment mind, can create total paranoia . . . at a minimum, this process will further erode the surface image of pseudo-democratic politics; at a maximum, it can lead to a closing of the convention — or a shortening of its agenda — for security reasons.[16]

Threats that appear less serious to an analyst (but not necessarily to the establishment) came from the Yippies. Whether the threats were serious or not, Chicago could not afford to ignore them, for the Yippies had succeeded in producing disruption at other times and in other places: In February, they had satirized a drug raid by police with a Yippie raid on the Stony Brook campus of the State University of New York. On March 21, they had held a "party" for about 5000 people in New York city's Grand Central Station. Both demonstrations had included some violence, for which the institutions had been unprepared. Some of the Yippie statements about Chicago were:

Be realistic, demand the impossible. An immediate end to the War in Vietnam [and a series of other serious demands]. . . . The legalization of marijuana and all other psychedelic drugs. . . . The total disarmament of the people, beginning with the police. . . . The abolition of Money. . . . We believe that people should fuck all the time, anytime, whomever they wish.[17]

We demanded such relevant things . . . [as] the abolition of pay toilets — that was one of our key items.[18]

[The Yippie demonstration] was a gesture to show that they felt they had to protect the convention. We didn't know they were going to do the thing with the barbed wire, but they played their roles perfectly.... Our mere appearance there, thousands of freaky looking people is in itself a disruption.... For example, when they knew we were running a pig, they put an armed guard on the pig in the zoo. It just made them look ridiculous. We wanted to make them look ridiculous because we felt they were.[19]

People will be attempting to use guerrilla theater techniques, people will be attempting to use satire, people will be attempting to talk to other people and people will be passing out newspapers, and some will be stoned and some will be fucking on the grass, and people will do whatever they want to do.[20]

There's no doubt about it. We're going to wreck this fuckin' society. If we don't this society is going to wreck itself anyway, so we might as well have some fun doin' it.[21]

We put a finger up their ass and tell them, "I ain't telling you what I want," then they got a problem.[22]

See you next August in Chicago at the Democratic National Convention. Bring pot, fake delegate's cards, smoke bombs, costumes, crud to throw and all kinds of interesting props, also football helmets.[23]

If the Central Committee gives us Humphrey anyway, then ... we can leave the country, we can drift into quietism and tend our private gardens, or we can disrupt, disrupt, disrupt.[24]

Cars and buildings will burn. Chicago may host a Festival of Blood.... There are many reasons to disrupt the Death Gala. If you feel compelled to cavort, then this is the action city.[25]

According to Chicago's own post-convention statements, the city took all these threats seriously. A 60-minute program produced for television, "What Trees Do They Plant?" and a booklet published by the city, *The Politics of Confrontation*, mention plans of the agitators to bring hundreds of thousands to Chicago.[26] These publications do not note that this specter of numbers appeared before Lyndon Johnson withdrew and before Eugene McCarthy and Robert Kennedy became serious contenders in the race for the nomination. Although only 10,000 agitators finally appeared, the city in its later statements attempted to justify its extensive preparation and eventual suppression by showing films of a small group of Yippies practicing some kind of blockading techniques and by displaying the weapons used by the agitators, a motley collection (and a relatively small one) of rocks, nails, knives, cans, bottles, and possibly an explosive.

Henry W. DeZutter, in "Politicians of the Absurd," briefly analyzes the city's justification:

> In a story written by the pseudonymous Malcolm W., "a member of the Chicago Black Power underground," *Saga* [a men's magazine] "told all" about "Black Guerrilla Plans to Smash the Democratic Convention." The article detailed the deadly weapons to be employed, including the dread "Chicago Cutter." "The Cutter," *Saga* said, "is constructed with ultra-thin balsa wood and a 1/16-inch sharp edge of a razor blade. It is to be placed under the sheets of a hotel bed … and is virtually undiscernible until the luckless hotel guest (read: delegate) slides between the sheets and slashes his entire body."
>
> To demonstrate the reliability of Malcolm W., he identified Rennie Davis, the son of a white Iowa agronomist and former 4-H leader, as a black leader "born in Panama."
>
> The Mayor's report [*The Politics of Confrontation*]—issued after the Convention to justify the police actions and "expose" the demonstrators—relies heavily on the *Saga* article. In fact, the article was the major "proof" that demonstrators intended to "disrupt the Convention and paralyze the city."[27]

Nonverbal offensive

Apparently, the Yippies decided to be in charge of nonverbal provocation. As one of them said, the very presence of these freaky-looking people was disruptive in a sense. The Yippies mounted the Pig for President campaign, which used such songs as "She's a grand old pig, she's a high-flying pig."[28] (Chicago arrested Pig on the basis of an ordinance prohibiting loose livestock in the city limits.[29]) Allen Ginsberg gained a considerable following with his "holy AUM" chant.[30] The Yippies raised what was apparently a Viet Cong flag on a general's statue in the park. The Yippies, or a few of them, practiced self-defense tactics in the park, possibly for the benefit of news media and police cameras. The Yippies probably brought the primitive weapons used extensively by the city in its post-convention statements. The Yippies also sponsored such activities as "Yippie Olympics, Miss Yippie Contest, catch the candidate [Pig], pin the tail on the donkey, pin the rubber on the Pope, and other normal, healthy games."[31]

Obscenity, verbal and nonverbal

The tactic that probably prompted the "police riot,"[32] the violent suppression witnessed by millions on television, was the use of obscenity.

Although we shall also mention token violence, we think that the violent confrontation of police and agitators would have occurred without it and that much of the agitators' violence was in response to police attacks and was defensive rather than aggressive.

Verbal obscenity was extremely common and clearly intended to be provocative. Nonverbal obscenity—symbolic, really, but also concrete—such as throwing at the police taboo or disgusting materials including feces, urine, and toilet paper was also common.

The following representative instances cited in the *Walker Report* illustrate agitation's provocative use of verbal and nonverbal obscenity:

A policeman on duty in front of the hotel later said that it seemed to him that the obscene abuses shouted by "women hippies" outnumbered those called out by male demonstrators "four to one." A common epithet shouted by the females, he said, was "Fuck you, pig." Others included references to policemen as "cock suckers" and "mother fuckers."[33]

Rolls of toilet paper were coming from the 15th floor.[34]

A guard official said later that his men were attacked with oven cleaner and containers filled with excrement.[35]

From within the crowd were rising the usual shouts from some of the demonstrators: "Hell no, we won't go!" ... "Fuck these Nazis!" ... "Fuck you, L.B.J.!" ... "Pigs, pigs, pigs!"[36]

A senator's driver noticed a group of demonstrators walking south, chanting: "Hell no, we won't go!" and "Fuck the draft!"[37]

A policeman on Michigan later said that ... a "female hippie" came up to him, pulled up her skirt and said, "You haven't had a piece in a long time." A policeman standing in front of the Hilton remembers seeing a blond female who was dressed in a short red minidress make lewd, sexual motions in front of a police line. ... Earlier in the same general area a male youth had stripped bare and walked around carrying his clothes on a stick.[38]

As the crowd moved south ... on Michigan, a traffic policeman, who was in the vicinity of Adams Street, recalls, "They first took control of the lions in front of the Art Institute. They climbed them and shouted things like, 'Let's fuck' and 'Fuck, fuck, fuck!'"[39]

There was sporadic violence in Old Town [Wednesday] night [when the greatest violence occurred]. Two University of Minnesota students who wandered through the park in the morning say they heard small groups of demonstrators saying things like "Fuck the pigs," and "Kill them all," but by this time that was not unusual.[40]

During the morning [Wednesday, before the major confrontation], Abbie Hoffman was arrested at the Lincoln Hotel Coffee Shop, 1800 North Clark, and charged with resisting arrest and disorderly conduct. According to Hoffman's wife, Anita, she and her husband and a friend were eating breakfast when three policemen entered the coffee shop and told Hoffman they had received three complaints about an obscene word written on Hoffman's forehead. The word was "Fuck." Hoffman says he printed the word on his forehead to keep cameramen from taking his picture.[41]

The obscenity cited was clearly an important element in the rhetorical escalation to violent suppression.

Eyewitnesses report that the police also used obscenity freely both as a prelude and as an accompaniment to the violence. The *Walker Report* quotes the following representative statements:

You'd better get your fucking ass off that grass or I'll put a beautiful goddam crease in your fucking queer head.[42]

You better get your fucking dirty cunt out of here.[43]

Move! I said, move, god dammit! Move, you bastards![44]

Get the hell out of here.... Get the fuck out of here.... Move your fucking ass![45]

Certainly these kinds of statements failed to calm any agitators.

That the obscenity was instrumental in producing violent confrontation is clear from post-confrontation statements by city officials. Typical explanations of police behavior pointed to the obscenity of the agitators, usually with a modest refusal to quote the language explicitly. After such a recital, Mayor Daley asked Walter Cronkite the rhetorical question, "What would you do, Walter?" Such a question implies that any normal American would react to obscenity with violence.

Token violence

As individuals, some agitators had consciously adopted a strategy of "Gandhi and guerrilla." They had come to Chicago expecting to attack the establishment physically. This was the highest step in the escalation of Chicago as far as the agitators were concerned. The physical attack consisted of behavior such as throwing rocks and chunks of concrete and displaying and using knives, razors, oven cleaner, and possibly explosives. These objects are weapons, not symbols. Furthermore, some agitators did attempt, hopelessly, to break through police lines. If massive police suppression had not been prompted by the lower-order rhetorical strategies (and it pro'>ably had been), this nonverbal, essentially nonrhetorical, series of attacks could have been depended on to bring about the violent confrontation.

Aftermath and Rhetorical Assessment

The events in Chicago prompted a flurry of communicative activity. We have already mentioned the city's movie and booklet justifying the behavior of the police and attributing the violence to "over-reaction" by a few. Apparently to counter these documents, the American Civil Liberties Union produced a film, "The Season's Change," and distributed a slick magazine, *Law and Disorder: The Chicago Convention and Its Aftermath.*[46] All these documents show substantial biases in the selection of evidence and its treatment, and a number of other such publications have been produced, including a satirical film by the Yippies. A commercially successful film, "Medium Cool," uses the confrontation as a backdrop. The events in Chicago also prompted the careful but outspoken *Walker Report,* which we have used as an authoritative collection of facts. More recently (November 1969), Vice President Spiro Agnew has publicly raised questions about the objectivity of the news media, citing, among other things, the radio and TV networks' coverage of the Chicago convention as being biased against the establishment.

The agitation has had other consequences. Seven of the agitators were tried in Chicago, charged with conspiracy to incite violence. They adopted the same rhetorical strategy in the court that they adopted in the streets, since they behaved in such a manner as to produce over-reaction on the part of the judge, Julius Hoffman. To some degree, this strategy succeeded: Judge Hoffman declared a mistrial for Bobby Seale after Seale, in the wake of several outbursts, had been forced to sit bound and gagged in the courtroom.

Politically, the agitation has been instrumental in producing a number of changes. The Democratic party has done away with the unit rule, thus making its delegates more responsive proportionally to the membership of the party. A few organizations, mostly academic ones, have declared their political convictions by canceling or moving to other cities conventions and conferences scheduled for Chicago. Among these organizations have been the American Sociological Association, the American Political Science Association, the American Psychological Association, the Modern Language Association of America, the American Historical Association, the American Association of University Professors, and the Speech Association of America. The Chicago demonstrations and other, later, confrontations made Hubert Humphrey a focus of controversy. In a period in which law and order are paramount to many Americans, this controversy may have been the factor that cost him the presidential election.

In Chicago itself, four policemen were dismissed, about forty others disciplined. Several policemen were indicted on civil rights charges resulting from disturbances at the convention, but the trend has been for juries to acquit those who have been tried.[47] The disturbances may also have had some effect on Chicago's political system. Donald Janson wrote in a *New York Times* story on March 13, 1969:

> Independent Democrats in special City Council elections upset today one candidate of Mayor Richard J. Daley's Democratic organization and forced another into a runoff April 8.
>
> Fred D. Hubbard, 40-year-old social worker with youth gangs, convincingly defeated Lawrence C. Woods in the overwhelmingly Negro Second Ward on Chicago's South Side. The vote was 6,942 to 4,599.
>
> Daley candidates won the four other seats, as expected....
>
> The Singer-Gaughan runoff now becomes a major test of strength between the Daley organization and party reformers.
>
> The organization has held the ward for a decade. Two years ago the organization's victory margin was 10,676 to 2859.[48]

The *Times* reported on April 9, 1969, that William S. Singer, the independent candidate, had narrowly defeated James P. Gaughan, the Daley candidate. We do not intend to imply that the agitation surrounding the convention was a direct cause of this reversal, but we do argue that it may have contributed to it.

Rhetorically, the agitators demonstrated considerably more sophistication than did the city. Mobilization and the Yippies predicted Chicago's reaction with remarkable accuracy. Ironically, however, most observers were most negatively influenced by police violence inflicted on the relatively conventional young people associated with Coalition, a group that took no part in the agitative planning.

We think that the city suffered, both actually and rhetorically, because of its intransigence. The control strategy of avoidance may have been wise from the city's point of view in the months preceding the convention. No doubt, that strategy did discourage some potential agitators from coming to Chicago. However, it also virtually assured that those who did not come would be the moderates, people who might have had a temperate effect on their more exuberant colleagues.

Certainly, once the agitators had arrived, some adjustment by the city would have been advisable if violence was to be averted. In fact, we find it surprising that Chicago had not learned a lesson from the 1964 Republican convention in San Francisco, where violence was also threatened and where law-enforcement policies were described as follows:

> We had decided to consider all this as similar to the conditions at a football game, where rooters are not necessarily arrested because they tear down the goal posts or are drunk. We treated it the same way—no arrests.[49]

The rationale for this policy was that the police should act as an interface between contending groups, not as a contending group themselves. According to Gordon E. Misner:

> In meeting with representatives of [agitative] groups, [Undersheriff] Pomeroy gave assurance that if arrests of demonstrators had to be made, there would be no rough handling on the part of the police. . . . The policy and the strategies developed apparently worked, for the Convention was not disrupted, constitutional rights had been protected by the police, and not a single arrest was made during the course of the Convention, not even of a drunken delegate.[50]

This San Francisco strategy of control was given further reinforcement when it was consciously and successfully adopted by the Washington, D.C., police during the inauguration of President Nixon in January 1969.

The control strategy in Chicago was quite the opposite of the San Francisco strategy. In Chicago, laws were strictly enforced for all potential agitators, and beatings, including beatings of newsmen, far outnumbered arrests. We agree with Tom Wicker's assessment:

> In fact, violence did not breed counter-violence in Chicago—not in any sense justifying what the police did. The antiwar demonstrators had sought for weeks to get permission for a peaceful march on the convention hall and a demonstration outside it. It is true enough that the most radical of the demonstrators' leaders wanted a "confrontation," but it was Daley and the police who forced it. Had they sought to control the demonstrators by cooperating with them and granting them elementary rights of marching and demonstrating, instead of repressing them by force, there need have been nothing like the brute spectacle millions of Americans witnessed on their television screen and that Humphrey could see from his hotel windows.[51]

If Chicago had adopted the more lenient strategy of adjustment to the agitators' means, of course, out-of-towners would have been permitted to sleep in the parks, minor violations of the law would have been winked at, and substantial concessions would have been made by the city concerning parade routes and the use of Soldier Field. These concessions would have freed the police to make arrests when actual instances of unprovoked physical aggression occurred. Control agencies would not have been placed in a highly defensive and sensitive situation in which wholesale violence was almost inevitable.

The agitators went some distance toward establishing the credibility of their syllogism:

Chicago acts as the United States acts.

Chicago acts brutally and oppressively.

Therefore, the United States acts brutally and oppressively.

August 1968 witnessed Chicago reacting to agitation in a brutal and oppressive manner. Furthermore, historical investigation reveals that this kind of reaction to agitation has been typical of Chicago for the past few years. The minor premise of the syllogism received substantial support as the result of Chicago's reaction to the agitation. The major premise— that Chicago is typical of the United States—is not so strongly supported. Analysis indicates that a number of cities in the United States—including at least San Francisco, Miami, Los Angeles, and Washington, D.C.—have sometimes adjusted much more peacefully and successfully to agitation than Chicago. Nevertheless, the agitators in their post-convention messages did produce some belief in the premise, especially when black people would testify that they daily witnessed in various ghettoes police aggression of the kind displayed publicly against the agitators in Chicago.

We do not anticipate a repetition of the Chicago affair in 1972 or, for that matter, in the foreseeable future. We think that the establishment will be forced to change the circumstances that provided agitation's ideology in 1968. If those circumstances do not change, agitation in later years is likely to take on guerrilla and revolutionary characteristics rather than the essentially rhetorical characteristics of escalation/confrontation. Even if circumstances in 1972 provide the ideological opportunity for a replay of the Chicago agitation, we think it unlikely that control will adjust as slowly and suppress as quickly and violently as Chicago did. The rhetorical successes scored by the escalation/confrontation strategy in Chicago are so expensive to the establishment's fund of legitimate and referent power that they are unlikely to occur again.

APPENDIX A

LIST OF EVENTS RELEVANT TO CHICAGO AGITATION

April 15, 1967. Representing 150 organizations, 100,000 people stage a peaceful protest march to the United Nations building in New York city. This march consolidates the leadership position of Mobilization.

October 21, 1967. Mobilization organizes a march of 50,000 people to the Pentagon. About 5000 of these are not peaceful.

October 1967. Mobilization begins planning for Chicago. Early hopes—with President Johnson as the focus of protest—are for about 100,000 demonstrators.

November 1967. The Yippies begin making plans for Chicago.

November 30, 1967. Senator Eugene McCarthy (Minnesota) announces his candidacy for the nomination for president.

Winter 1967 and Spring 1968. Dick Gregory makes statements about leading a mass demonstration of blacks at the convention in Chicago.

December 18, 1967. Mobilization's administrative committee (about 70 people) meets to discuss Chicago. Rennie Davis reports "loose talk," no specific plans.

January 1968. The Yippies begin to plan for their Festival of Life.

January 1968. Mobilization meets with the National Lawyers' Guild.

Tom Hayden says at the meeting: "We should have people organized who can fight the police, people who are willing to get arrested." Another speaker says: "We have to have two hats—nice and violent."

January 1968. A convention planning committee is formed within the Chicago Police Department. It meets biweekly through the spring and summer, evaluating the situation, gathering intelligence from informants, and making plans.

February 1968. New York Yippie leader Jerry Rubin gets in touch with The Chicago Yippies. They announce plans for the Festival of Life in Chicago, including "a gaint music fair, a nude-in on the beach, workshops of various sorts, including draft resistance, use of LSD, underground newspapers and other matters uniquely of interest to the dropout community. There would be poetry sessions, information exchanges, political forums and a convention of underground intellectuals to discuss the direction of a new society."

February 1968. Mobilization makes Rennie Davis its Chicago coordinator. He is to work closely with Tom Hayden.

February 1968. Yippies stage a mock narcotics raid on the Stony Brook campus of the State University of New York. Some violence results.

February 11, 1968. Mobilization meets in Chicago with representatives of black groups, SNCC, CORE, and NRO (National Rights Organization). The black groups make no commitments. A meeting of all interested groups is set for March 22–24.

March 12, 1968. Senator McCarthy achieves unexpected victory over President Johnson's stand-in in New Hampshire, the nation's first primary election.

March 16, 1968. Senator Robert Kennedy (New York) announces his candidacy for the presidential nomination.

March 21, 1968. Yippies stage a "party" in New York's Grand Central Station. Some violence results.

March 22–24, 1968. Lake Villa, Illinois, is the scene of a meeting of Mobilization with other interested groups, including Yippies. Three Yippie leaders—Abbie Hoffman, Jerry Rubin, and Paul Krassner—say they expect tens, maybe hundreds, of thousands to come to Chicago for the Festival of Life. However, no real plans come out of the conference. It is suggested that the blacks have parallel demonstrations with Mobilization and allied groups, culminating in a combined "funeral march" to the

Chicago Amphitheater, site of the convention. Some organizations, including Students for a Democratic Society, tell the conference that they are not interested in mass demonstrations in Chicago. Rennie Davis and Tom Hayden make a grandiose statement of what might happen, still expecting President Johnson to win renomination. Davis is quoted as saying that the demonstrators might do best "by closing down the city." But the black groups do not follow up, and soon afterward Mobilization's administrative committee meets in Washington only to postpone decisions about Chicago.

March 31, 1968. President Johnson announces that he will not accept his party's renomination.

April 4, 1968. Dr. Martin Luther King is assassinated in Memphis. His violent death prompts extremely destructive riots in Chicago's black community. After a night of chaos, Mayor Daley contradicts police regulations by saying that officers should "shoot to kill arsonists and shoot to maim looters."

April 27, 1968. Vice President Hubert Humphrey announces his candidacy for the presidential nomination.

April 27, 1968. In Chicago, 6500 people demonstrate for peace in Vietnam, marching to the Civic Center. There police disperse them with excessive force (clubbing), according to eyewitnesses and a subsequent investigating commission.

May 10, 1968. Abbie Hoffman is in Chicago to make Yippie plans. The Chicago group of Yippies decides to dissociate from the New Yorkers, the Chicagoans naming themselves The Free City Survival Committee. This group negotiates with the city of Chicago to arrange for the Festival of Life.

June 5, 1968. Robert Kennedy is assassinated.

June 19, 1968. Mayor Daley meets with representatives of the National Guard.

Summer 1968. Various groups negotiate with the city of Chicago for parade permits and permission to sleep in parks.

July 20, 1968. Mobilization meets in Cleveland, makes first firm plans for Chicago.

July—August 1968. Mobilization makes various statements, all vague; has set no dates for various demonstrations. Some in Cleveland wear STOP

THE CONVENTION buttons, but Rennie Davis disclaims any attempt to literally disrupt the convention. New York commitments to go to Chicago are disappointing to Mobilization leaders, one spokesman estimating ten or fifteen thousand, an estimate labeled by the Walker Commission as "wildly optimistic." (Only about one thousand finally made the trip.)

Early August 1968. Yippies from New York meet with their Chicago counterparts. Jerry Rubin and Abbie Hoffman make aggressive, violent statements about what will happen. Chicago group warns others through their newspaper (*Seed*) that they should not come to Chicago during the convention expecting to have fun. The Yippies still do not have permits for their planned activities.

August 5, 1968. The city of Chicago begins to act on applications for permits. Mobilization has applied for a parade permit for 150,000 people. Mobilization also wants some of these to be permitted to sleep in the parks. Yippies have similar applications in. On this date, the city of Chicago refuses the applicants permission to sleep in the parks, saying that it will enforce an 11 P.M. curfew.

August 10, 1968. Senator George McGovern (South Dakota) announces his candidacy for the presidential nomination.

August 12, 1968. Senator McCarthy requests that those who support his candidacy stay out of Chicago during the convention.

August 20, 1968. Governor Shapiro of Illinois announces that the National Guard (11,000 troops) will be mobilized during the convention to aid Chicago's 12,000-man police force.

August 21, 1968. Chicago refuses permits to march to the Amphitheater or around the downtown hotels. The city proposes alternative routes unacceptable to Mobilization and Yippies.

August 23, 1968. Judge William J. Lynch dismisses an appeal from the city's judgment not to issue permits. Disaffected protesters march to Daley's office, but the mayor is not in.

August 25–29, 1968. The Democratic convention.

August 27, 1968. The city of Chicago issues a permit for an afternoon rally by Mobilization the following day in Grant Park.

APPENDIX B

BIOGRAPHICAL SKETCHES OF A FEW SPOKESMEN

Mayor Richard Daley. An Irish family man who rose through the ranks of the party machinery and takes pride in maintaining his home in the same lower-middle-class neighborhood in which he was born. Mayor Daley has been popular with the business community, extremely powerful in Illinois party politics, and a kingmaker of a sort in national politics. He helped significantly in the nomination and election of John F. Kennedy in 1960. His statements during and after the convention made him seem a fortress of middle-class values. The fortress metaphor may help account for his position of power in a period of social turbulence.

Mobilization spokesman David Dellinger, 52. A native of Wakefield, Massachusetts, a *magna cum laude* graduate of Yale, member of Phi Beta Kappa, winner of Henry Fellowship for study in England. Dellinger served two prison terms during World War II for refusing to serve in the Army, although he could have been deferred from service as a student at Union Theological Seminary. He had visited Hanoi and Cuba twice and organized meetings with North Vietnamese and NLF in Czechoslovakia. During November 1967 he was one of 14 members of the War Criminal Tribunal which met in Denmark to hear charges that the American forces in Vietnam were guilty of war crimes.

Mobilization spokesman Rennie Davis, 28. Holds a political science degree from Oberlin College and a master's degree in labor and industrial relations from the University of Illinois. In 1965, after one year of graduate study at Michigan, he went to New York, where he worked as a community organizer for SDS. In the summer of 1967, he traveled to North Vietnam, and joined the Mobilization Committee on his return. He had experience with community organizing in Chicago, where he helped to form JOIN (Jobs or Income Now), a project aimed at organizing Appalachian whites in the Uptown area, concentrating on housing and welfare problems. He was a planner at the Center for Radical Research and an organizer of the Resistance Inside the Army (RITA). Davis was a principal participant in the New Politics Convention in Chicago, where he gained a reputation for his theory of building local organizations as bases for militant political action.

Mobilization spokesman Tom Hayden, 28. Born in Michigan, he graduated from the University of Michigan, where, in his senior year, he was editor of the *Michigan Daily.* During the summer of 1961, he worked on the summer project of SNCC in Mississippi. In 1962, he went to Port Huron, Michigan, where he was a founder of SDS and authored the Port Huron Statement, as well as the SDS by-laws and constitution. He helped organize the Newark Community Project, a community union similar to JOIN. In 1965, he traveled to Hanoi with Herbert Aptheker and Staughton Lynd. In early July of 1968, he went to Paris for two weeks to consult with the North Vietnamese. He was reportedly active in the Columbia University agitation during the spring of 1968.

Yippie spokesman Jerry Rubin, 30. A former Cincinnati newspaper reporter, later active in the pro-Maoist Progressive Labor Party in California. He participated in organizing the march on the Pentagon in October of 1967, and was involved in various demonstrations in Berkeley. He seemed to have a tendency to associate with demonstrations that turned out to be violent. However, he was also reported to have been one of the sponsors of the April 1967 peace demonstration in New York, which was not violent.

Yippie spokesman Abbie Hoffman, 31. Had been active in agitation for some time. Once a psychologist, he left his job to participate in civil rights demonstrations in the South. Along with Rubin, he had participated in demonstrations in Berkeley, New York, and at the Pentagon.

Notes to Chapter 4

1. Robert Perrucci and Marc Pilisuk (editors), *The Triple Revolution: Social Problems in Depth* (Boston: Little, Brown, 1968), page vii

2. Daniel Walker, *The Walker Report to the National Commission on the Causes and Prevention of Violence: Rights in Conflict* (New York: Bantam Books, 1968), page 14; hereafter referred to as *Walker Report*

3. City of Chicago, *The Strategy of Confrontation: Chicago and the Democratic National Convention—1968* (Chicago: City of Chicago, 1968), page 4

4. *Liberation*, November 1967; quoted in *Walker Report*, page 88

5. *Chicago Daily News*, January 6, 1968; quoted in *Walker Report*, page 89

6. Abbie Hoffman, "Why We're Going to Chicago," in Walter Schneir (editor), *Telling It Like It Was: The Chicago Riots* (New York: The New American Library, 1969), page 13

7. City of Chicago, *op. cit.*, page 47

8. Informant's report of an anonymous speaker at a Mobilization meeting, January 26, 1968; quoted in *Walker Report*, page 30

9. Report of August 4, 1968, Mobilization meeting, *Walker Report*, page 40

10. *New York Times* quotation of Rennie Davis, March 24, 1968; quoted in *Walker Report*, page 35

11. Quotation from Dave Dellinger, *Guardian*, August 17, 1968; quoted in *Walker Report*, page 35

12. *Chicago Tribune*, December 31, 1968; quoted in *Walker Report*, page 88

13. *Chicago Tribune* quotation of an anonymous delegate to a National Conference for New Politics meeting, December 31, 1967; quoted in *Walker Report*, page 89

14. Quotation from Rennie Davis in a Mobilization document, February 1968; quoted in *Walker Report*, page 89

15. *Walker Report*, page 37

16. Tom Hayden on *Ramparts* Wall Poster, August 25, 1968; quoted in *Walker Report*, pages 36—37

17. Yippie flyer, quoted in *Walker Report*, page 44

18. *Walker Report*, page 48

19. Paul Krassner, quoted in *Walker Report*, page 45

20. Abbie Hoffman, quoted in *Walker Report*, page 42

21. Abbie Hoffman, quoted in *Walker Report*, page 43

22. *New York Free Press*, quoted in *Walker Report*, page 46

23. *Village Voice* quotation of Jerry Rubin, November 16, 1967; quoted in *Walker Report*, page 88

24. *Village Voice*, June 20, 1968; quoted in *Walker Report*, page 90

25. *Seed* quotation of Free City Survival Committee, August 1968; quoted in *Walker Report*, page 91

26. City of Chicago, *op. cit.*, pages 4—7

27. Henry W. DeZutter, "Politicians of the Absurd," in Donald Myrus (editor), *Law and Disorder: The Chicago Convention and Its Aftermath* (Chicago: Donald Myrus and Burton Joseph, 1968), distributed by American Civil Liberties Union; no page numbers. The apparent dependence on *Saga* is also referred to in *Walker Report*, page 98

28. Yippie post-convention movie

29. *Walker Report*, page A-6

30. Allen Ginsberg, "Public Statement Presented at the Chicago Coliseum, August 27, 1968," in Walter Schneir (editor), *op. cit.*, page 107

31. "Daring Expose—Top Secret Yippie Plans for Lincoln Park," quoted in *Walker Report*, page 83

32. *Walker Report*, page 5

33. *Walker Report*, page 235

34. *Ibid.*

35. *Walker Report*, page 238

36. *Walker Report*, page 243

37. *Walker Report*, page 244

38. *Walker Report*, page 248

39. *Walker Report*, page 277

40. *Walker Report*, page 279

41. *Ibid.*

42. *Walker Report*, page 237

43. *Ibid.*

44. *Walker Report*, page 253

45. *Ibid.*

46. Donald Myrus (editor), *op. cit.*

47. Associated Press, September 23, 1969

48. Donald Janson, "Daley Man Defeated in Chicago; Another Is Forced into a Runoff," *New York Times*, March 12, 1969, page 28

49. Joseph Kimble, "Patience and Planning: The Key to Controlling Demonstrations," *Law and Order* (September 1965), page 48; quoted in Gordon E. Misner, "The Response of Police Agencies," *Annals of the American Academy of Political and Social Science*, CCCLXXXII (1969), 118

50. Misner, *ibid.*

51. Tom Wicker, "The Question at Chicago," quoted from the *New York Times* in Walter Schneir (editor), *op. cit.*, page 58

Chapter five

UNEASY TRUCE: SAN FRANCISCO
STATE COLLEGE, 1968–69

At the very time Americans were becoming accustomed to reports of yet another campus demonstration, television viewers on Tuesday, December 3, 1968, witnessed a savage and chilling spectacle of students and police on the brink of violent conflict. San Francisco State College, allegedly one of the most liberal and progressive public institutions in the country, was convulsed in the throes of the longest and most successful student strike the United States had ever known. The Black Student Union (BSU) and the Third World Liberation Front (TWLF)—supported by white students, faculty, and some organized labor groups—had created an agitative movement that at one time kept more than 9000 students away from class and more than 2000 persons on the picket lines. (San Francisco State then had a student body of about 18,000.) Other statistics are provided by William H. Orrick, Jr., in his staff report to the National Commission on the Causes and Prevention of Violence:

> The campus became the first to be occupied by police on a continuous basis over several months, and it was only the daily presence of 200 to 600 policemen which kept the college open from the start of the strike on November 6 to the end of the fall semester. Even so, the campus had to be closed on three occasions during late 1968. By the end of the semester on January 31, 1969, there had been 731 arrests on campus; more than 80

students were reported injured as they were arrested, and others were hurt and not arrested. Thirty-two policemen were injured on campus. Damage to campus buildings exceeded $16,000; there were scores of small fires and a major one in the vice president's office. Eight bombs were planted on campus, and two firebombs were hurled at and into the home of an assistant to the president.[1]

Boycotting a class or a professor or a school dates back at least to the medieval universities of Paris and Bologna. But a strike—essentially a labor tactic developed to force employers into negotiations—had never been used on such a scale by students in the United States before the San Francisco State College incident. Several agitative forces and decision-making agencies contributed to the strike, and, to appreciate the rhetorical strategies used by each group, one needs an understanding of these forces and agencies. The following diagram will serve to indicate both the relative power and the ideological positions of the various agitative and control factions and the organization of the following analysis.

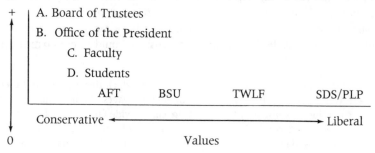

Background

California has a unique system for providing higher education to its youth. According to the state's Master Plan, those in the top 12% of their high school graduating classes may attend one of the nine campuses of the prestigious state university. Those in the upper third may go to one of the eighteen state colleges. Others may elect a junior college. A Board of Regents with constitutional status governs the university; a Board of Trustees, subject to abolition by the state legislature, controls the colleges. Serving both as a trustee and as a managing executive is a chancellor whose office gathers and disseminates information for the Board of Trustees.

Campus autonomy in matters of personnel and academic programs is practically nonexistent. Moreover, the state colleges operate on a line-item system of budgeting, whereas the university receives a lump-sum budget. This line-item system—together with a two-year lag in the budget and no contingency fund—results in financial inflexibility. Several years ago, for example, the chancellor underestimated the amount needed for faculty salaries by 1.8% and, although funds in other line-items were unused, the faculty were simply not paid 1.8% of their salaries. To create or expand programs within colleges, therefore, a campus must re-order its own priorities. For example, an increase in the staff of a black-studies program means either *no increase* or a *decrease* in the staffs of other programs and departments. Any reordering of priorities, of course, creates ill-will and dissension among departments.

Too, the 10,000 faculty members of the state college system have no single agency to represent them. An academic senate does serve as a faculty voice, but depends on the Board of Trustees for its annual appropriations. The American Federation of Teachers (AFT) represents a minority of the faculty, but was twice rejected by the Trustees as a bargaining agency. Even if the faculty did have a single representative agency, it is unlikely that the Board of Trustees would enter into meaningful negotiations:

> They [the Board] believe there is no way in which they can commit themselves to a binding agreement involving wages, hours, and working conditions because only the legislature can provide funds to back up such an agreement. Second, they feel they cannot negotiate with a group which represents only a portion of the faculty because California's Brown Act requires them to meet and confer with *any* employee organization to discuss conditions of employment. They argue that it is impossible for them to meet with any group for the purpose of working toward the conclusion of a binding agreement which would, in effect, foreclose other groups from discussing the same issues with the trustees.[2]

Against a backdrop of unresolved problems such as these, we need to explore the ideologies of the groups within the vertical distribution of legitimate power prior to the agitation.

The Ideology of the Establishment

The board of trustees

Sixteen members appointed by the governor for eight-year terms and five ex-officio members make up the decision-making body of the California

state college system. One writer asserted that the Board members represented "at least six banks, three newspapers, two oil companies, three
aircraft manufacturers, two shipping lines, three airlines, half the food
packing industry of California, a half dozen real estate and insurance firms,
several chain stores, and two giant utilities."[3] In general, the members
believe in maintaining the Master Plan for California's educational
system. As a consequence, they are committed to a policy that emphasizes
teaching rather than research at the state colleges. From their decisions
during the strike we may infer that they believe in a rigid concept of law
and order at the expense of legitimate dissent, if necessary. Since they
depend entirely on legislative appropriations for financing the college
system, they tend to be responsive to the wishes of the state government.
Governor Reagan, elected on a platform of returning morality, fiscal
responsibility, and peace to the campuses and the state, serves as an
ex-officio Board member. As Governor, his powers of enforcement are considerable; as Board member, his decisions tend to be heard and heeded.
Moreover, the majority of the trustees were appointed by Governor
Reagan. A brief biographical sketch of each member of the Board of
Trustees is provided in Appendix A of this chapter.

The office of the president

Referring to the presidency of San Francisco State College, William
Orrick notes:

> The college has had seven presidents since 1960; three in less than 6 months
> during 1968. Presidential succession, occurring once or twice in a decade
> under normal circumstances, can cause serious problems of adjustment in a
> college or university; to have seven presidents in 8 years is tantamount to
> having no presidential leadership at all.[4]

To complicate matters further, each person occupying the office prior
to the strike used a markedly different style of leadership. President
Glenn Dumke, later chancellor of the college system, tried to increase
campus autonomy. President Paul Dodd seemed reluctant to engage in
campus politics. President John Summerskill took office in September
1966, and instead of delegating authority to subordinates, tended to make
most decisions personally. As a result, faculty grievances were channeled
directly to his office rather than to the faculty senate. In coping with an
SDS boycott of the student cafeteria and several antiwar protests, President
Summerskill apparently sided with the trustees, thereby losing much of his
personal influence with the moderate students on campus.

On November 6, 1967, a group of black students entered the offices of the *Gator*, San Francisco State's student newspaper. The editor, James Vaszko, was beaten; office equipment was destroyed. Although the Black Student Union denied responsibility for the attack, a *Gator* photographer had pictures of the assault.

A few days later, the black students turned themselves in in response to warrants for their arrest. One of them was George Mason Murray, co-ordinator of the student-run ghetto tutorial program, and a graduate student who held a part time teaching assistantship in the English department. President Summerskill announced the suspension of Murray and three others, pending disciplinary action.[5]

The attack on the *Gator* staff and a subsequent publication of an obscene poem by another campus newspaper, *Open Process*, caused many politicians to call for more strict disciplinary action by Summerskill. A coalition of SDS and BSU protested the president's disciplinary action by occupying the administration building, and despite considerable destruction (which was televised), no police were called in. In an emergency meeting of the trustees, Summerskill was publicly criticized for his failure to use police to curb the demonstration. More important, the Board of Trustees passed a resolution whereby each campus president had to appoint a person to maintain "constant and effective liaison with outside police agencies to assure that these forces are ready to come onto campus at any time with their maximum amount of available force."

In effect, President Summerskill was deprived of any discretion in using coercive and legitimate power. Some referent power, however, still resided with him. At their next meeting, his faculty gave him a four-to-one vote of confidence, recorded its objection to the trustees' resolution, and began concerned discussion of the "erosion of local control"—a key complaint of the later AFT strike.

In February Summerskill resigned and gave as his reason political interference in the educational system.

In April the trustees tried to increase the numbers of minority students able to attend state colleges. The attempt failed for lack of funds. And, although he had resigned, Summerskill did exercise his power by appointing Nathan Hare to develop a black-studies program. Then there developed a protest against military recruitment on the campus, and many California politicians called for stricter control. Arrests, beatings, and disruption ensued. Summerskill's staff sharply disagreed with the concessions he made to the protesters, and the semester ended.

Inheriting a position of attenuated power, Robert Smith, head of the education department, accepted the presidency of the college. One writer described the new president's ideology in this way:

> Smith was also a liberal. But he was older, less inclined to make extravagant statements. He was a careful diplomat, was popular with the faculty and therefore seemed the ideal man for the presidency. With such deep discontent on campus, Smith's role was not so much to make everyone happy again, as it was to prevent another explosion.[6]

Shortly after the fall semester began, Smith's legitimate power was further eroded by the Murray incident. Newspapers in San Francisco and Los Angeles reported that George Murray—participant in the *Gator* beating, Black Panther, visitor to Cuba, and antiwar militant—was teaching at San Francisco State. Murray had been suspended as a graduate teaching assistant and later reinstated by Summerskill, who had assured Murray's department chairman that he would institute disciplinary actions against Murray. Summerskill, however, failed to act in the Murray case. Although "there was no criticism of Murray's teaching; nor was there any indication that he ever used his classroom for political purposes," President Smith was asked by the trustees to reassign Murray to a nonteaching position. To acquiesce would alienate his faculty; to refuse would be to invite the trustees to increase their control of the college. While Smith stalled to gain time, Murray made a series of inflammatory speeches, telling his audience at one point:

> Political power comes from the barrel of a gun. If you want campus autonomy, if the students want to run the college, and the cracker administrators don't go for it, then you control it with the gun.[7]

Despite strong pressure from the chancellor and the trustees, Smith held to his dilatory policy and did not suspend Murray until October 31. Predictably, the faculty was incensed at the dismissal, with its blatant disregard for academic freedom and due process. On the same day the BSU announced their intention to strike.

The faculty

As we have indicated, the teaching staff at San Francicso State could be characterized as liberal. They believed in making education relevant to social issues, and they repeatedly demonstrated their willingness to experiment with new programs and educational innovations. Unable to agree on a single group to represent their beliefs to the trustees, they nevertheless did maintain that the principles of academic freedom and due process were necessary for their college. Unable to communicate their position to the trustees except through the academic senate, the president, and the chancellor, they had reason to believe that legitimate power was being taken from them. Academically and financially they considered themselves second-class citizens when compared to the teaching staffs at the university campuses.

Some evidence of faculty ideology can be inferred from the strike issues that were later made by the San Francisco State chapter of the American Federation of Teachers. A complete list of these issues is reproduced in Appendix B of this chapter. However, some key issues deserve mention here. In addition to demands for more money and staff, the thrust of the document is to regain legitimate control of the college. They asked for clearly defined regulations concerning grievances, personnel policies, professional activities, and faculty involvement in all decisions concerned with academic and administrative matters. The AFT strike demands indicate that many of the faculty believed that, in order to regain power in the college, they needed legitimizing contracts with the trustees.

Students

Of the 18,000 students at San Francisco State, only 3% are housed on campus. Of those who enter, only 33% remain to graduate. In 1968, 76% of the students were white, 5% black, 2% Mexican-American, 8% Oriental, 1% Indian, and 1% Filipino. (The remaining 7% did not answer the college's official ethnic survey.) What these statistics do not reveal is that California's three-track system of higher education had contributed to a decline in minority enrollment at the universities and four-year colleges. Despite the fact that the San Francisco area has a 50% minority race population, few minority students were able to meet the entrance requirements at San Francisco State. Although citizens in the community were paying high taxes to support California education, their sons and daughters were being forced by the Master Plan to attend inferior junior colleges, only to discover two years later that they were still unable to qualify for admission to the state colleges or the various branches of the university. Many San Francisco area students believed that the inequity had to be resolved.

"Students see themselves," one writer said, "as noble people fighting battles to uplift the nonwhite races and promote reforms or revolution that will produce a better way of life. Officials who slow down or interfere with this process are branded enemies of the people."[8] Students at San Francisco State also had considerable economic strength. In 1967 they controlled a budget in excess of $500,000, which was used to support athletic programs, student publications, theaters, tutorial programs, the Black Student Union, etc.

Just a week before the strike began, 6000 students expressed their belief in a form of self-determination. These students petitioned the trustees to accept plans for a new student union, financed by student funds. Designed by Moshe Safdie, an internationally recognized architect, the proposed building would meet a need for a meeting place on campus. The trustees rejected the design first because they perceived the building as "ugly, impractical and incompatible with the campus architecture," and later on the grounds that parts of the proposed building did not meet standard safety regulations. Accustomed to being treated as responsible adults, many students prior to the strike believed their legitimate requests were being unfairly denied by a remote group of decision-makers motivated, in large part, by politics. Despite continued administrative rebuffs, many students did not support the agitative group of strikers. Whether these nonstriking students supported the Board of Trustees cannot be determined.

The Ideology of the Agitators

The ideologies of the major agitative groups are somewhat less clear than that of the establishment groups.

The American Federation of Teachers (AFT) believed that teachers should have the power to negotiate wages and teaching conditions with the college administration.

The Black Student Union (BSU) believed in black power, which initially emphasized black culture and pride. Later, they began to articulate a program of revolutionary politics. Before the strike they were divided on the question of integration, but convinced that San Francisco State was essentially a racist institution. The BSU believed that blacks needed their own identity, separate from the whites, and built on a positive cultural conception of their intrinsic worth. They believed that education in the United States perpetuated myths of equality "that the power structure wants perpetuated and therefore is detrimental to black people who seek the truth."[9] Prior to the strike, they generally believed that the best method for attaining their goals was working within the system. Their single act of destruction (the *Gator* beating incident) had cost the BSU a certain amount of support from the white students; thus the BSU did not participate in the spring 1968 demonstrations. The BSU demands for more black studies and more black admissions were quite well developed "long before the suspension of Panther English teacher George Murray."[10]

The Third World Liberation Front (TWLF) was formed in the spring of 1968. Led by Roger Alvarado, this organization also believed in "the need to restructure American society so that it is more responsive to the needs of their ethnic groups."[11] Composed of six member groups, TWLF was a loose federation designed to secure measures to meet the educational needs of minority students. The organization had engaged in a partially successful demonstration prior to the strike:

> TWLF staged its first major action in May of 1968, demonstrating for a week to support a series of demands that included 400 special admissions for Third World students in the fall of 1968, retention of Dr. Juan Martinez, an activist Mexican-American professor, and financial assistance to guarantee that any students admitted under the special program would not have to drop out because they needed money.
>
> They won that fight, although the college filled only a little more than half of the special admissions slots for reasons that are in dispute but center around a shortage of the necessary funds.[12]

During the strike, TWLF made five additional demands, some of which were later accepted. (See Appendix C of this chapter.)

Two other groups, the Students for a Democratic Society (SDS) and the Progressive Labor Party (PLP) were actively engaged in the strike. They considered the main issues of the strike to be racism and the class nature of the university sytem. Moreover, they believed that revolution was necessary to change the system. A recent SDS publication expresses their ideology:

> SDS is a mass student organization that fights against the war in Vietnam, against racism, and has increasingly allied with workers against the big businessman who oppress both workers and students.
>
> We think students have a common interest with workers. More than half of all college students fail to graduate, and most of those who do graduate become teachers, social workers, nurses, etc., who suffer low wages and bad working conditions like all working people. They therefore have

an interest in uniting with workers to fight back. The war, furthermore, hurts workers more than students, and workers are in a more powerful position to stop it—it is they who can shut down the whole show![13]

An uneasy alliance existed between TWLF and SDS. Third World leaders welcomed support only so long as the issues were not confused, but they exercised no control over tactics used during the strike. Nonetheless, SDS and PLP did support the strike.

Strategies of Petition and Avoidance

On October 31, 1968, the BSU released the following demands to the press:

1. That all Black Studies courses being taught through various other departments be immediately made part of the Black Studies Department, and that all the instructors in this department receive full-time pay.
2. That Dr. Nathan Hare, Chairman of the Black Studies Department, receive a full professorship and a comparable salary according to his qualifications.
3. That there be a Department of Black Studies which will grant a Bachelor's Degree in Black Studies; that the Black Studies Department, the chairman, faculty and staff have the sole power to hire faculty and control and determine the destiny of its department.
4. That all unused slots for black students from Fall, 1968 under the Special Admissions Program be filled in Spring, 1969.
5. That all black students wishing so be admitted in Fall, 1969.
6. That twenty (20) full-time teaching positions be allocated to the Department of Black Studies.
7. That Dr. Helen Bedesem be replaced from the position of Financial Aids Officer, and that a black person be hired to direct it, that Third World people have the power to determine how it will be administered.
8. That no disciplinary action will be administered in any way to any students, workers, teachers, or administrators during and after the strike as a consequence of their participation in the strike.
9. That the California State College Trustees not be allowed to dissolve the Black Programs on or off the San Francisco State College campus.
10. That George Murray maintain his teaching position on campus for the 1968–69 academic year.

On November 1, President Smith sent a memo to faculty and students declaring that: "We will not condone violence and will take whatever steps are required to meet disruptive or violent action with responses calculated to insure safety of individuals and property."

On November 6, the strike began, with token violence. In terms of our theoretical model of rhetorical strategies and tactics, both agitation and control moved too quickly into confrontation and suppression. A more precise appraisal, however, would need to consider the petition/promulgation which preceded the beginning of the strike. Students had gone through proper channels to secure a new union building; their requests were denied with the rationale of "unsafe design." Teachers had petitioned through recognized channels to secure higher wages, a more reasonable teaching load, disciplinary procedures, etc. Some of these petitions were denied for legitimate reasons of insufficient funds. Others were simply denied. Still others were in the process of being adopted when the strike began. The control tactic of evasion—probably unintentional but nonetheless effective—was vividly described by TWLF leader, Roger Alvarado:

> We did a tremendous amount of homework on a proposal for minority studies, laid out sketches, curriculum, instruction, all laid out to meet special needs of the groups involved. Then we began going around to different offices trying to institute some of these courses within the curriculum. What we got was incredible. Even people who thought that the course was a good idea would say, "Well, you should have had this in six months ago because that's when a decision was made." You get a real crossfire of information. You go to someone's office, they tell you to go elsewhere. You go there, this cat explains how this function is really a little different from what that cat said, so he can only do this much for you, you got to go somewhere else . . . it's the way the institution is laid out, man. Anyone can do whatever he wants to as long as he doesn't make any changes in the institution.[14]

Frustration and a willingness to accelerate the means needed to bring about reforms were probably occasioned by such intentional or unintentional avoidance strategies prior to the strike.

In fact, when the strike began on November 6 with a confrontation between 300 white radicals and President Smith, he responded with more avoidance strategies rather than using suppression. While roving bands of students were entering classrooms, small fires were breaking out, and office equipment was being destroyed, Smith elected to postpone any administrative reaction by closing the school, saying, "This is not the time or place" to discuss strike demands. We maintain that avoidance tactics from control are inappropriate when agitation elects to use confrontation and guerilla strategies. Any delay from the decision-makers of the establishment gives an agitative group more time to solidify and gain adherents to its ideology. Two days after the BSU demands were given to Smith, the TWLF presented its own list of five nonnegotiable demands. Favored by an establishment unwilling and unable to quell the token violence, rumors of greater violence directed against nonstrikers quickly spread.

Making these rumors more credible were booklets like *Your Manual*, which were widely distributed to strikers and nonstrikers alike. This seven-page, spirit-duplicated document proclaimed that "The oppressor's cancerous hands are around our throats and they will only release them when he sees his own blood on the earth."[15] The "manual" then devotes a page to "Basic Equipment for Rallies and Other Battles with the Pigs," suggesting such apparel as crash helmets, brass knuckles, construction boots, crotch protection cups, and the like. Three pages give detailed instructions for purchasing components and assembling several types of homemade bombs. An additional two pages specify the "Supplies, Ordinance, and Logistics" recommended for the militant strikers:

II.   SUPPLIES, ORDINANCE, AND LOGISTICS

A. *Rocks and Bottles*

Throwing either of the above can be very effective if they are thrown by numbers of rebels. An empty bottle or a rock can disable a pig for a whole campaign.

1. *Supplying Personnel*
Before rallies rocks or bottles should be brought on campus by as many people as possible. Students should fill purses, lunch bags, book bags, pockets, and attache cases full of rocks and while strolling around the campus grounds he/she can casually drop the rocks or bottles in strategic locations. eg. 1 rally area 2 streets 3 walkways 4 off campus near intersections.

2. *Throwing Rocks or Bottles*
a) Before you throw any rocks or bottles observe if there are any pig cameramen on top of buildings. If there are any on the roofs throw at them first. No pictures will be taken if they are driven off.
b) During any disruption the scabs always are. at the windows watching the pigs beating the shit out of the people. They, the pig scabs, are also good targets.

c) When throwing at the pigs aim at their midsection or necks. They all wear helmets.

If you can identify scab cars throw at them when no other prime targets are available.

B. *Red Pepper, darts, water guns etc.*

1. Red Pepper can be very effective against mounted pigs. Always try to position yourself so you can throw the pepper downwind into the horses faces (?). If you hit your target the pig may end up on his ass, where he belongs.

2. *Darts*

Should be thrown at the horse's body, not the pig because the horse is the easier target. Advantage is darts are easily concealed, and disposed of.

3. *Water Guns*

Fill guns with regular household ammonia (NH_3) and squirt in horses eyes and face. If all goes well pig again ends up on his fat ass.

4. *Cherry bombs*

To be effective they must have bb's and tacks glued onto the cherry bomb's surface. These horses are trained against noise but not against pain.

C. *Ice Picks, leather punches, can openers*

1. *Ice picks & Leather Punches & Can Openers*

Used to best advantage on car tires of scab "teachers," "students" and "administrators". Scratches paint jobs nicely too. Very good on plain clothes pigs too.

D. *Sling Shots*

1. Buy a "Wham O" sling shot at your sports store or department and a package of marbles. Very good on windows and pigs on roof. Sling shots can be used at long range and with more power thus you are safer and do more damage to the pigs than you might otherwise do. Highly recommended.

E. *Picket signs*

1. A 1" × 2" or larger or a broom or ax handle make very good clubs or at least defensive weapons to block clubbing pigs. If you wish

you may want to sharpen the end of the club to have a more versatile weapon. You may use the spear to stab or throw at oncoming pigs.

F. *Steel & Lead Pipe, black jacks & chains*

G. *The Mace*
   1. This weapon has been used by the "VC" very effectively. If thrown hard enough it can drop a fully armed pig.
      a) hard ball sized rock
      b) mud or clay
      c) nails
      d) another layer of clay and mud to secure nails

H. *Sugar*
   1. Pour one cup sugar in gas tank of scab car. It may be one more person is deterred from going to class.

I. *Spray Paint*
   1. For those artistically inclined. Spray on windshields and bodies of scab cars.

J. *Zippo* cigarette lighter
   1. This little device has been very successfully used by our enemies in Vietnam (the U.S. military). We ignite curtains, waste baskets, and bulletin boards, or paper towel in bathrooms.
   2. Can of *lighter fluid* can be used in conjunction with the Zippo lighter to increase effectiveness of the effort.

K. *Oven Cleaner* in aerosol can to be used as a weapon doing severe damage to any exposed skin area of the enemy.

L. *Eggs, Tomatoes and Ink Bottles* use fruit against enemy and ink against property.

Documents such as *Your Manual* had two immediate effects. First, the number of students and faculty who stayed away from the campus out of fear rather than sympathy could be *claimed* by agitation as sympathizers. Physical absence, as we noted in Chapter 2, can be an effective tactic of nonviolent civil disobedience. More important, however, is the fact that, when physical absence *symbolizes* beliefs and is used as an *instrument* to secure social change, it is rhetorical. No doubt many students and faculty did not appear on campus for fear of encountering the weaponry described in *Your Manual*. Their absence, nonetheless, could be interpreted by the strikers as evidence of solidarity and high actual membership. And although the college administration could (and did) issue statements saying that estimates of the success of the strike were inflated, the message of empty classrooms remained. Only by legitimizing the empty classrooms— i.e., closing the college—could the administration reduce the impact of the physical absences. Yet, from a control point of view, closing the college meant tacit acceptance of the agitative groups' goal, namely, that racist institutions be stopped.

Strategies of Confrontation and Suppression

On November 12 a faculty meeting passed a resolution censuring Chancellor Dumke for firing George Murray without academic due process. The following day proved to be the turning point of the strike.

The campus was closed, 65 members of the AFT joined the strike, and at noon an SDS rally was underway while George Murray held a press conference at BSU headquarters, a small hut located near the center of the campus. A cameraman was beaten and a nine-man unit of the San Francisco Tactical Squad was sent to a nearby building to investigate. Two plainclothesmen accompanied the cameraman to the hut area and somehow lost radio contact with the uniformed Tac Squad. Fearing that the plainclothesmen were in trouble, the squad marched to the BSU area.

Vice President for Academic Affairs Donald L. Garrity describes the ensuing melee:

> There is the Tac Unit, and black students with all of their feelings about not only the police but the Tac Unit. We have a frightened kind of situation.
>
> They blew it right then and there. Flat out mistake on the part of the police. With all of the symbolism that's involved for black people and the like, in this movement. The Tac Squad comes in and somebody yells, "There's the Tac Squad."[16]

Hundreds of students from the SDS rally raced to the BSU hut, where the surrounded and outnumbered police proceeded to fight their way out. Another Tac Squad began fighting inward from the periphery to rescue their fellow officers, and a full-scale riot was on. Faculty members finally placed themselves between the students and police, thereby allowing the officers to leave. That afternoon President Smith ordered the campus "closed until further notice."

The November 13 riot was intended by neither agitation nor control. True, the rumors of violence, the incendiary rallies, token violence, official evasion and postponement had set the stage for violent conflict. Clearly President Smith, with his woefully inadequate legitimate power, had tried to resolve ideological differences with minimum force, and clearly the strike had been effective prior to November 13. Intended or not, however, both sides made rhetorical capital of the violent incident.

While the strikers recruited previously uncommitted students and faculty, the college administration received an attack from within. Governor Reagan said the order to close the college was "an unprecedented act of irresponsibility" and demanded that the campus be reopened "with dispatch." "As long as I am governor," he said, "our publicly supported institutions of higher education are going to stay open to provide educations for our young people."

An establishment must have a cohesive ideology and considerable referent power to successfully withstand attacks on the institution from without. At San Francisco State most of the faculty neither liked nor trusted the Board of Trustees and wanted the campus closed in order to reassess their educational approaches. President Smith wanted the campus closed temporarily to consolidate his faculty and, through a series of conferences and convocations, gradually reopen the campus. The Board of Trustees met and ordered the campus opened. Smith resigned.

There can be little doubt that from a control viewpoint Smith was sacrificed by way of adjusting to the strike. In order to defeat the striking agitators, the college had to be kept open. In order to keep the college open, the Board needed a representative in the presidency who would be willing to use massive doses of coercive power if necessary. S. I. Hayakawa, semanticist and professor of English, was appointed acting president on November 26.

The issues of the strike were more clearly drawn when Hayakawa declared on November 30 a "state of emergency" on campus. Under California law such a declaration enables a college to use police if and when needed. Although he was armed with considerable legitimate and coercive power (the trustees had given him increased financial and manpower aid) President Hayakawa lacked a reservoir of referent power. Orrick, for example, notes that Hayakawa's ability "to obtain the good will of political leaders and the public at large appeared directly inverse to his lack of success at reaching his campus constituency."[17] The news media, knowingly or unknowingly, provided the new acting president with an off-campus base of referent power. Hayakawa describes the event:

> When, on December 2nd, I sort of blew my top and climbed that sound truck and pulled out those wires it just happened that all the media were there. And after that dramatic incident, right to this day, television people, and radio people, and newspaper people are after me constantly because that incident made me a symbolic figure. And so, like any other symbolic figure, you're good copy, you're always news just because you're there.
>
> It wasn't anything planned. That was the luckiest thing that ever happened to me—that sound truck incident. It just suddenly, you know, just placed power in my hands that I don't know how I could have got it if I wanted it.[18]

Although the basic issues of the strike were far too complicated for the general public to understand, the picture of an elflike professor bravely and physically defying a mob of militant demonstrators polarized outside support for Hayakawa. In effect, then, he no longer needed—nor did he rely on—faculty or student support in responding to the strike, since he had a sympathetic following outside the campus.

Beginning on December 3 (later known as "Bloody Tuesday"), guerrilla tactics were countered with violent suppression strategies. When rocks were thrown, police batons were used and arrests were made. When the striking group increased in size with the addition of black community leaders and the AFT, Hayakawa closed the college early for a Christmas recess. During the holidays a superior court ordered the Associated Students' funds placed in receivership, thereby denying some militants the means of agitation.

Further efforts were made to deny the strikers the means of promulgating their ideology and solidifying their membership when Hayakawa announced:

> With only four weeks left in this semester we all have a lot to do if courses are to be successfully completed and credit granted. In view of the foregoing the period beginning January 6 and extending through January 31 is hereby declared to be a limited activity period. Specifically, rallies, parades, be-ins, hootenannies, hoedowns, shivarees, and all other public events likely to disturb the studious in their reading and reflection are hereby forbidden on the central campus.[19]

Agitation received further support, however, from the Central Labor

Council, which gave official sanction to the AFT strike. In effect, all work on campus performed by union employees stopped: deliveries, garbage collection, electrical repair, and other services. Many observers claimed that this sympathy strike probably did more to make the college administration willing to negotiate than any other single factor.

Those on strike repeatedly met superior force, but no brutal beatings. At one rally in January strikers were ordered to disperse. They refused, only to find a police cordon around the entire group. Four hundred arrests were quickly made without injury. Significantly, Nathan Hare, strike leader and black-studies chairman, was among those arrested. With their ranks decimated, the campus blanketed with police, and the semester nearly over, the strikers declared a "tactical victory." A "Mexican stand-off" would have been a more appropriate term.

From the beginning of the strike, efforts at adjustive resolution had been tried. San Francisco's mayor, Joseph Alioto, and the Central Labor Council tried to mediate the grievances between the Teachers' Union and the Board of Trustees. In February the AFT teachers voted to return to work after the trustees agreed to accept a new grievance procedure. The BSU continued to man the picket lines, but much of their support was gone. They tried to solidify their membership with leaflets (see Appendix D of this chapter), but they were unable to re-escalate to the strike's former intensity. In March Acting President Hayakawa announced a settlement with the BSU.

> The administration granted the major demands of the striking students for a minority curriculum and for the admission of more minority students. The administration agreed to set up a School of Ethnic Studies, part of which will be the Black Studies Department, it being understood that the admission policies at the School of Ethnic Studies and the staffing be nondiscriminatory. The administration declined to continue the employment of Nathan Hare or to rehire George Murray.[20]

And San Francisco State pledged itself to try to change the admission quotas so that more minority students could be admitted.

Aftermath and Rhetorical Assessment

Shut It Down: A College In Crisis included a section entitled, "Outlook for the Future." We have reproduced this section in Appendix F of this chapter. For a time almost all student body funds remained frozen, judicial procedures against many student demonstrators were pending, and faculty resignations increased 25% in 1969 over 1968. In May 1969 a faculty grievance and disciplinary action panel recommended that Hayakawa be severely reprimanded and removed from office for ignoring the wishes of the faculty during the strike. In June he was made President. When the fall 1969 semester opened, a grading scandal was discovered: During the strike 33% of all grades earned by students were A's, which resulted in a mean grade-point average of 3.22. In 1964, it had been 2.57. The Western Association of Colleges, the area's accrediting agency, extended San Francisco State's accreditation by only two years instead of the usual ten.

We argue that the agitators did secure short- and long-term effects with their strategies of petition and brief nonviolent resistance. Public attention was focused on the social and racial injustices and, we believe, public sympathies ultimately favored the BSU position. Each strategy carries its risks, however, and although we fully understand the need for continued promulgation and the need to secure greater support, we believe that incorporating avowedly militant and revolutionary ideological positions into the ranks of agitation eventually nullified the effects of any short-term gain in numbers. The divergence of beliefs and values between the revolutionaries and the moderate liberals who supported the decision-making agency became unnecessarily magnified. Also, employing token violence creates a climate of fear among moderates, as well as sometimes prompting the hoped-for overkill from control agencies. Fear is most easily removed by removing the cause: in this instance, those on strike and their supporters.

The agitators used indiscriminately far too many flag issues and flag persons. The issues of racism and minority education became blurred when other issues of alleged brutality, faculty grievance procedures, teaching loads, student funds, etc., were added. Also, cohesive strength was diluted by deprecating first Summerskill, then Smith, then Hayakawa, then Reagan, and, finally, the trustees. In some cases the flag person was too remote, in others a control tactic of sacrificing personnel easily blunted any gains made from using flag persons as a rallying focus. That the BSU/TWLF were able to sustain a strike of such length suggests to us that a broad, unified ideological base of support already existed. If and only if they use their collective organization to petition peacefully and reasonably for continued social reforms can we say that the strike was a successful rhetorical agitation. They have demonstrated their strength, and apart from myopic violence, they did make their grievances and ideology known to a wide audience. To move from awareness to realistic adjustment requires patience, compromise, and dignified determination.

Control, in our judgment, lost the rhetorical encounter. Avoidance tactics were used far too long and far too openly, thereby giving agitation both time to solidify and more demonstrable grievances. Reluctance to suppress an agitation is almost as detrimental to control as reluctance to adjust to the agitative ideology, because the delay itself is an ambiguous message to the agitators. Not knowing whether their grievances are being resolved in good faith or rejected in secret, and not knowing whether more agitative force is needed, agitation usually responds by escalating. The evidence presented by the San Francisco State College incident suggests that the BSU escalated their tactics precisely because they did not know where their proposals were in the decision-making machinery. Moreover, the evidence clearly suggests that control was not expecting the worst to happen, despite a three-year history of agitative incidents. No consistent ideology, no clearly defined disciplinary mechanism, little referent power, and almost no legitimate power was given to the college decision-makers except as temporary expedients during the strike. Realistic adjustments, made early, would have prevented the encounter as effectively as the protracted and much more costly banishment tactics.

APPENDIX A

BOARD OF TRUSTEES OF THE CALIFORNIA STATE COLLEGES*

EX OFFICIO MEMBERS

Ronald Reagan, B.A., Governor of California
Robert H. Finch, B.A., LL.B., Lieutenant Governor of California
Max Rafferty, Jr., A.B., M.A. Ed.D., State Superintendent of Public Instruction
Jesse M. Unruh, B.A., Speaker of the Assembly
Glenn S. Dumke, A.B., M.A., Ph.D., LL.D., L.H.D., Chancellor

APPOINTED MEMBERS

(The term of each trustee expires on March 1 of the year indicated in parentheses. Terms are 8 years.)

Mrs. Philip B. Conley, B.A. (1972), Fresno
Native of Sacramento; wife of Judge Philip Conley, Fourth Appellate District Court of Appeals; mother of James McClatchy, William E. McClatchy, Charles K. McClatchy, and Philip P. Conley; civic and community leader in Fresno; graduate of Vassar.

---

*From *Shut It Down: A College in Crisis*, A Report to the National Commission on the Causes and Prevention of Violence, by William H. Orrick, Jr.

Alec L. Cory, B.A., LL.B. (1973), San Diego
President, San Diego Bar Association; appointed Deputy City Prosecutor; named Rationing Attorney for the Office of Price Administration; senior partner in law firm of Procopio, Cory, Hargreaves and Savitch; member of the Charter Review Committee of the city of San Diego; served on the education committee of San Diego's Chamber of Commerce; completed a term as president of the UC Alumni Club of San Diego County.

George D. Hart, A.B. (1975), San Francisco
President, George David Hart, Inc.; trustee, Ross School District; Director, Constantin, Ltd., of London, Liberty Mutual Insurance Co. of Boston, Liberty Mutual Fire Insurance Co., and Mutual Boiler Insurance Co.; past President, San Francisco Library Association; former memebr of the San Francisco Art Commission; member of the Board of Governors, San Francisco Employers Council.

Louis H. Heilbron, A.B., LL.B., LL.D. (1969), San Francisco
Attorney at law; trustee, World Affairs Council of Northern California, Newhouse Foundation, and University of California International House; past president, San Francisco Public Education Society, and State Board of Education; chairman of trustees, 1961–63.

Earl M. Jorgensen (1970), Los Angeles
President of Earl M. Jorgensen Co., steel products distributing firm; serves on the Board of Directors of Northrop Corp., Transamerica Corp., American Potash & Chemical Corp; and Hollywood Turf Club; member of board of trustees of California Institute of Technology; charter member of University of Southern California and Pomona College Associations; member of St. John's Hospital Board of Regents; past director of YMCA of Los Angeles, Junior Achievement of Los Angeles County, and California Chamber of Commerce.

Edward O. Lee, B.A. (1974), Oakland
Occupational department chairman of the East Bay Skills Center in Oakland; former Oakland High School teacher; served as business agent for the American Federation of Government Employees, Local 1533; served on Human Relations Commission and was on the Equal Opportunities Committee; past member of the Oakland Adult Minority Employment Committee; past president of Oakland Federation of Teachers, Local 771; member of the executive board of the Central Labor Council of Alameda County.

Charles I. Luckman, LL.D., A.F.D. (1974), Los Angeles
President, Luckman Associates, Architects; former president of Lever Brothers; served on Presidential Commissions on Equality of Treatment and Opportunity in the Armed Services, on Metropolitan Area Problems and Chairman of Food Commission; Director, Southern California Symphony Association; president of Los Angeles Orchestra Society; chairman of trustees, 1963–65.

Theodore Meriam, A.B. (1971), Chico
Department store manager and vice president and director of Lassen Savings and Loan Association, Chico; former mayor of Chico; past President, League of California Cities; formerly Chairman, Chico State College Advisory Board. Received honorary master's degree, Chico State College, 1959.

William A. Norris, B.A., LL.B. (1972), Los Angeles
Attorney at law; served as member and vice president of State Board of Education and board's representative on State's Coordinating Council for Higher Education; named special counsel to President Kennedy's commission on airlines in 1961; served as law clerk to Justice William O. Douglas during 1955–56 term of the U.S. Supreme Court; worked on the California-Arizona Colorado River litigation; member of American, California, and L.A. County bar associations; partner in Los Angeles law firm of Tuttle and Taylor.

Daniel H. Ridder, B.A. (1975), Long Beach
Copublisher of Long Beach *Independent-Press Telegram*; director and vice president of Twin Coast Newspapers, Inc.; Director, U.S. National Bank of San Diego; former publisher of St. Paul *Dispatch, Pioneer-Press*; past president of Western Conference of Community Chests, United Funds, and Councils; past president of Long Beach Community Chest; director, Bureau of Advertising of the American Newspaper Publishers Association; Chairman of Advisory Board of St. Mary's Hospital of Long Beach.

Albert J. Ruffo, LL.B., B.S. in E.E. (1971), San Jose
Teacher, engineer, and attorney; member of Tau Beta Pi and Woodsack Engineering and legal honor societies. Former vice president, Board of Governors, State Bar of California; member of American Bar Association and American Judicature Society; former City Councilman and mayor of San Jose; former member of faculty, University of Santa Clara; assistant football coach, Santa Clara, Calif., and 49ers; chairman of trustees, 1965–67.

Paul Spencer, B.A. (1969), San Dimas
Citrus rancher and president, Sycamore Groves, Inc., former general contractor; former building inspector for Los Angeles City School System; former project engineer for Federal Public Housing Administration; director, San Dimas Lemon Growers Association and San Dimas Orange Growers Association; director, Reliable Savings and Loan Association, West Covina, served as member and president of Bonita Union High School board of trustees; past president of Alumni Association of Occidental College; past director of Southern California Chapter of Associated General Contractors.

Dudley Swim, A.B., M.A. (1976), Carmel Valley
Chairman of Board of National Airlines; Director of Providence Washington Insurance Co.; previously appointed to Coordinating Council for Higher Education; Trustee of Rockford College, Ill., Wabash College, Ind., Cordell Hull Foundation for International Education, Free Society Association; former director of Fremont Foundation; member of advisory board of Hoover Institution on War, Revolution and Peace; a director of Stanford Research Institute; president of Monterey County Foundation for Conservation; previously served as national vice commander of American Legion.

James F. Thacher, A.B., LL.B. (1970), San Francisco
Partner in the San Francisco law firm of Thacher, Jones, Casey & Ball; Director of Actors Workshop and Neighborhood Centers of San Francisco; served on the California Toll Bridge Authority, the Commission on the Disposition of Alcatraz Island, and on the budget study committee of Northern California's United Crusade.

E. Guy Warren, B.A. (1973), Hayward
Owner, Warren Trucking Co.; member of Executive Board of California Trucking Association; member, Alameda County Fair Board of Directors, Alameda County Mental Health Advisory Board, and trustee of Hayward Union High School District; former president of California Trucking Association; past president of Western Highway Institute.

Karl L. Wente, M.S. (1976), Livermore
President of Wente Brothers Winery, Wente Farms, and Wente Land and Cattle Co.; director of Automobile Association, Livermore Valley Memorial Hospital, Livermore Water District, and the Livermore branch of Bank of America. He is a Stanford University graduate.

APPENDIX B

STRIKE ISSUES OF THE SAN FRANCISCO
STATE COLLEGE AFT, LOCAL 1352

I.   Strike Issues Directed to the President and Administration at San Francisco State College

A. Negotiation of and adoption of comprehensive rules and regulations governing:

1. Grievance procedures related to faculty affairs.

2. Personnel decisions (hiring, firing, tenure, promotion, demotion, suspension, lay-off).

3. Conditions under which pay can be reduced or docked.

4. Sick leave and other fringe benefits.

5. Unit and class load assignments for full and part-time faculty.

6. Stipulation of prerogatives and delineation of authority at various administrative levels.

7. Guidelines and standards for professional perquisites (sabbaticals, travel, research leaves).

8. Faculty involvement in decisions on academic matters (curriculum selection, assignment of faculty and staff, grading, graduation requirements, determination of calendar, admission requirements).

9. Faculty involvement in decisions governing all local administrative matters (office space, parking).

10. Recovery of faculty positions bootlegged for administrative purposes.

B. Protection of constitutional rights

1. Amnesty for all faculty, students, and staff who have been suspended or have been subject to other disciplinary action and/or arrested, and withdrawal of outstanding warrants as a result of activity to end racism at San Francisco State College.

2. No disciplinary action for exercising constitutionally protected rights.

C. Black Students Union and Third World Liberation Front grievances must be resolved and implementation assured.

D. All agreements on the above to be reduced to a written contract.

II. Strike Issues Directed to the Trustees of the California State Colleges

A. All agreements made with the local administrations under (I) above shall be binding upon and accepted by the Trustees.

B. Sufficient funds shall be provided from current reserve and emergency funds to:

1. Maintain the present faculty positions (this will prevent the lay-off of 100–125 faculty in the spring semester, 1969).

2. Gain new positions to replace those given by various departments and schools to staff a Black Studies Department and a School of Ethnic Studies.

3. Protect the revised work loads presently scheduled in many departments for spring, 1969, and assure the same for everyone who requests it.

C. Rescission of the ten disciplinary rules passed by the Trustees on November 26, 1968.

D. Approval of the Student Union plan presented by the Associated Students at San Francisco State College.

E. Cancellation of proposed changes in Title 5 that would take away student control of student body funds.

F. Recognition of college constitution that emerges from the Constitutional Convention called by the Academic Senate at San Francisco State College.

III. Strike Issues Directed to the Governor and the Legislature

A. That a special joint committee of the California State Assembly and Senate be appointed to conduct negotiations with the State College Board of Trustees and the Union to agree on systematic and continuing financing for the proposals under I and II above and to provide the necessary increases in salary required to maintain a qualified faculty at San Francisco State College.

B. That when the special Legislative Committee, the Board of Trustees, and the Union have reached agreement, the Committee report to the next session of the Legislature so that necessary monies may be provided to put the agreement into effect.

APPENDIX C

THE FIVE TWLF DEMANDS

1. That a School of Ethnic Studies for the ethnic groups involved in the Third World be set up with the students in each particular ethnic organization having the authority and control of the hiring and retention of any faculty member, director and administrator, as well as the curriculum in a specific area of study.

2. That fifty (50) faculty positions be appropriated to the School of Ethnic Studies, 20 of which would be for the Black Studies Program.

3. That in the spring semester, the college fulfill its commitment to the nonwhite students by admitting those that apply.

4. That, in the fall of 1969, all applications of nonwhite students be accepted.

5. That George Murray, and any other faculty person chosen by nonwhite people as their teacher, be retained in their positions.

APPENDIX D

WHY THE "PEACE TALKS" FELL THROUGH *

You have seen men who will pat you on the back to get you set up so that they can stab you in the groin. Such a man is S. I. Hayakawa, the renowned puppet of Ronald Reagan and the conservative right-wing power structure in this state.

Not long ago, he set up a so-called "select committee" supposedly empowered to engage in peace talks with strike leaders toward implementing the demands.

It soon became clear, however, as the committee vacillated and procrastinated all week long, that it was just another deceptive device, a cunning trick to prevent the Strike from regaining its natural momentum (after the semester break and the first week of getting enrolled for the second semester) by dangling false hopes of impending settlement before the strikers' faces.

We realized that Hayakawa could always veto the committee's agreements, just as he has vetoed his powerful Council of Academic Deans and Vice President Donald Garrity in the past. And so, inasmuch as we had

---

*Leaflet issued by the Black Students Union at San Franciso State.

always maintained that we would talk only to persons with power to implement the demands, we sent them a note:

> We now see very clearly your intentions are to vacillate, waste as much time as possible, and engage in unprincipled dialogue. For these and other reasons, we find it imperative that you answer each precondition either yes or no ... the select committee must either show that they have the power to meet all the demands, or have the necessary people present who can implement them ... That all disciplinary hearings on campus for striking students be dropped ... That George Murray must be immediately released from jail to participate in these meetings, or that the meetings must take place in the San Francisco County Jail.

They sent us a counter-precondition demanding that we call a "moratorium" of the strike while the talks were in progress. We replied that we would gladly comply provided that they declare that there will be no classes taught on or off campus meanwhile.

The Committee hedged all weekend, night and day, claiming that they were seriously working toward meeting the preconditions and had good expectations of doing so. Then, Sunday evening about six o'clock they sent us a shrewdly worded letter replying in the negative, saying, among other things, that they were "not empowered" to meet the preconditions.

Indeed, the chairman of the committee, Pig Curt Aller, reached back thirty years for a model, suggesting that we pattern ourselves after "the American workingman of thirty years ago."

We do not intend to go backward, never, and we are sorry that we let ourselves be tricked even momentarily into slowing down the struggle for our just demands. But that is done. Let us now strike on till victory is won.

APPENDIX E

THE OUTLOOK FOR THE FUTURE*

The story of San Francisco is an unfinished story. The teacher strike and the student strike have ended, the violence has subsided, and an uneasy peace prevails. But the deeply rooted problems which underlie San Francisco State's crisis—and which plague many of the country's higher education institutions—remain to be solved. Among these problems are long standing social and economic injustices and inequities and the reluctance of the so-called establishment to respond rapidly to the need for change.

The patience of those adversely affected has been over-estimated. The student leaders in controversy with the administration were prepared to go to direct confrontation in order to change the systems and beyond that to violence.

Sizable numbers of students and faculty, augmented by elements in the community as the action built up, were willing to follow this leadership. When people do not feel for their safety and such direct-action strategy is used, violence is a virtual certainty.

---

*From *Shut It Down: A College in Crisis,* A Report to the National Commission on the Causes and Prevention of Violence, by William H. Orrick, Jr.

The violence mirrors the turmoil, the sharply divergent outlook, and the economic and social imbalances which bitterly divide the American people today. It is misleading to attribute the causes of violence to outside agitators. The causes lie much deeper. The ugly consequences of violence have obscured the major reasons for the disorders and have obstructed the way to peace.

San Francisco, justly proud of its tolerance, will not permit property destruction or personal assault as a justification for "getting attention." San Francisco State cannot and should not become "surrogate" for the whole of San Francisco's social and economic ills. As has been said so often, an educational institution is of necessity fragile and is not built to withstand direct and violent attacks aimed at its heart.

Today at San Francisco State the groups involved in the conflict for the most part are polarized. The students are committed to their struggle as no generation of students has ever been. The faculty is fragmented, often unhappy, and increasingly militant over its rights and responsibilities. The administration is charged with the duty to manage, but is essentially powerless to act, caught between the conflicting pressures of the other groups. Trustees of the State colleges are determined to take a stand at San Francisco State; it has become for them a watershed of decision, the crucial point as they see it in a struggle for the preservation of the institutions of higher education.

The political leaders and the public at large are bewildered and angry over the turmoil and violence on the campus, at San Francisco State and elsewhere. But the issue will not be disposed of simply by saying that many people do not like it. The fact is that the "New Left" openly espouses violence as a key tool in the drive to lock the academic community securely into the general struggle against the community at large. It indicts all higher learning as the uncritical servant of business and the military, rather than helping the poor and the uneducated to advance. It seeks, in extreme form, the destruction of higher education and its visible institutions as they are presently constituted.

Californians are disturbed all the more because they have taken great pride in their publicly supported colleges and universities and have generously supported their more than 100 junior colleges, State colleges, and universities. Ultimately the progress—indeed the survival—of California's public institutions of higher learning depends upon broad-based public support. Operating funds require legislative appropriations, and capital expansion is financed through the issuance of bonds which require approval by the voters of the State. These are political and economic facts of educational life in California.

In the final analysis, the State colleges must therefore respond to the voting public. But the degree of response they should make, and the degree of insulation which the method of governance should afford them, are vitally important questions raised by the crisis at San Francisco State.

The present reevaluation of aims and purposes of education at San Francisco State must be pursued vigorously. On the part of the administration, patience, firmness, and recognition of curriculum deficiencies will be needed. On the part of the student leadership and their faculty supporters, there must be lasting recognition that the language of the gutter, the shock rhetoric, a willingness to "mount the barricades," vandalism, and personal assault do not constitute a valid or effective means of getting better education for themselves and their followers.

The Study Team talked with State legislators in an attempt to assess political reaction—and thus to some degree public reaction—to the turmoil at San Francisco State. Because disorders were occurring on other campuses, particularly at the neighboring Berkeley campus of the University of California, the reaction goes beyond San Francisco State.

The legislators interviewed are Democrats and Republicans, liberals and conservatives. For all of them, campus unrest is an immediate and important issue. Uniformly, they feel that the legislature must make some response to demonstrate its political credibility to the voters. Their views of the public attitude differ sharply. The more liberal of the legislators see the public response as a rejection of the new doctrine that colleges and universities should be powerful "relevant" agencies for social change, rather than instruments for indoctrination in the traditional wisdom. The most conservative see the public reaction as a justifiable response to a coercive effort by radicals to impose their views on the majority. Where one legislator sees the unrest as a struggle for Negro manhood, another sees only "creeps" and "bums" agitated by a hard-core preaching revolution imported from Cuba.

A special committee has been created by the State assembly, consisting of members of the Criminal Procedure Committee and the Education Committee; the combined membership will hear bills relating to campus conduct—more than 50 of which have already been introduced.

Liberals and conservatives alike agree that some form of legislation regulating campus conduct through criminal sanction will pass in this session. They feel it is a political imperative notwithstanding the recognition among most of those interviewed that, realistically, there is nothing the legislature can produce which will give college administrators and law enforcement authorities any greater legal foundation than they already have for dealing with conduct on the campus. Nor do most of those interviewed believe that the new criminal legislation will aid in solving the causes of the violence.

It is unlikely that there will be any reduction in appropriations for higher education in general. The education committee in the assembly has already begun work on a $2 million supplemental appropriation necessary to prevent enrollment cutbacks at the State colleges. While there were some urgings in the last session that the legislature punish the dissidents by cutting back college and university funding, most of the legislators believe that they should continue to reflect a general attitude among California's voters that education is "good," and that it would be inappropriate to deal with the disorders by reducing appropriations.

It seems equally unlikely that there will be any substantial increase in support for higher education. The legislators keep a sharp eye on the political weather vane. The voters rejected a $250 million bond issue for higher education construction in the November 1968 election. The bond issue lost, and it lost badly; only a few counties supported the measure. The Governor did not support it. One University of California official, knowledgeable about the bond issue's defeat, attributed the loss to two things: campus unrest and a general taxpayer's revolt. (In a number of local elections, voters have rejected proposals for tax-rate increases and bond issues to finance public schools.)

Special programs, such as the Educational Opportunity Program (EOP), may suffer. The Governor vetoed appropriations for the EOP from the State colleges' 1968—69 budget, and a trustees' request for more than $2.4 million in EOP money was not included in his budget for 1969—70.

Faculty salaries are the area most vulnerable to attack. Several legislators expressed the opinion that there might be no salary increase. There is a feeling that the few teachers who went out on strike acted irresponsibly, and their actions may be the cause of the legislature's refusal to provide more money for salaries. In view of the fact that economic parity for faculty salaries has been a prime issue with the teachers, it would be ironic if the strike were ultimately to retard the upward progress of faculty salaries.

Notes to Chapter 5

1. William H. Orrick, Jr., *Shut It Down: A College in Crisis*, A Report to the National Commission on the Causes and Prevention of Violence (Washington, D.C.: U.S. Government Printing Office, 1969), pages 1–2; hereafter referred to as *Report*

2. *Report*, page 13

3. Bruce Johnson, "Bread and Roses Too," *The Daily Iowan* (June 10, 1969), page 2

4. *Report*, page 17

5. *Report*, page 22

6. Steve Toomajian, "An Overview: The Strike at SF State," *Crisis at SF State* (San Francisco: Insight Publications, 1969), page 6

7. *Report*, page 33

8. *Report*, page 5

9. *Report*, page 88

10. Alex Foreman, "San Francisco Police State College," *The Movement* (January 1969), page 2

11. *Report*, page 100

12. *Report*, pages 100–101

13. *New Left Notes* (October 15, 1969), page 4

14. *Report*, page 101

15. *Your Manual* (published by "3" R News Service, Inc., San Francisco), page 1

16. *Report*, page 43

17. *Report*, page 58

18. *Report*, page 59

19. *Report*, page 62

20. *Report*, page 70

Chapter six

NONVIOLENT RESISTANCE: BIRMINGHAM, ALABAMA, 1963

Background

On December 1, 1955, Mrs. Rosa Parks, a strong-willed Negro seamstress, violated the law and custom of Montgomery, Alabama, by refusing to give up her seat on a city bus to a white person. The incident led to her arrest and subsequently to many other arrests when the Negro community of Montgomery decided to boycott the city buses in a direct protest against the company's segregationist policies. The policy stipulated that Negroes take seats in the rear of all buses and give up their seats when a white person could not find a seat. The boycott was extremely effective, since the bus system depended heavily on Negro patronage. After almost a year of boycott and litigation, the United States Supreme Court ruled on November 13, 1956, that segregation of the races in buses was unconsitutional.[2] Montgomery buses were desegregated, though not without bitterness and reprisals.

Much more important in the long run than this immediate effect were two other effects of the boycott: (1) A Montgomery minister had been elected to leadership in the Montgomery struggle. His name was Martin Luther King, Jr. (2) Under Dr. King's leadership, the boycott demonstrated the feasibility of nonviolent resistance and nonviolent civil disobedience. With only a few exceptions, the civil rights movement took this as its principal strategy of agitation for the following decade.

This strategy was a significant shift for civil rights advocates. Previously, except for sporadic and unorganized protests, the Negro community had depended for progress mainly on the National Association for the Advancement of Colored People, an organization that had been committed to legalistic solutions to civil rights problems. The NAACP, through petition and litigation, had made some gains, notably in the 1954 Supreme Court decision outlawing segregation in the public schools. The Montgomery boycott demonstrated to many that petition alone was too slow a process to be a practical solution for the many grievances of the American Negro. Thereafter, even the NAACP officially joined in a number of agitations involving nonviolent resistance.

The Southern establishment did not leap at the chance to desegregate all bus facilities. The rest rooms and waiting rooms in most train and bus depots remained segregated. In protest against the establishment's recalcitrance, a movement known as the freedom rides began. An integrated group would board an interstate bus in a Northern state, ride into the South, and attempt at each stop to violate the segregation enforced in waiting room, rest room, and restaurant facilities. In May of 1961, such a freedom ride reached Birmingham, Alabama, bringing into national focus Birmingham's Commissioner of Public Safety, Eugene (Bull) Connor, who epitomized the Southern establishment's response to nonviolent resistance.

Frequently, freedom riders would encounter hostility from the residents of cities whose bus depots were the targets of their agitation. Sometimes the agitators were arrested, but more often the police simply ignored them, leaving the task of suppression to vigilante-type mobs. This tactic of police avoidance and mob suppression was especially flagrant in Birmingham, where, according to Gordon E. Misner, "the greatest violence took place."[3] On May 14, 1961, white mobs brutally treated a group of freedom riders. The police were conspicuously absent.

The *Birmingham News*, which had supported Connor for Commissioner of Public Safety, attacked the inaction of the police editorially. It and national news media pressed Connor for an explanation. He is quoted as saying:

> I regret very much this incident had to happen in Birmingham. I have said for the last 20 years that these out-of-town meddlers were going to cause bloodshed if they kept meddling in the South's business.

It happened on a Sunday, Mother's Day, when we try to let off as many of our policemen as possible so they can spend Mother's Day at home with their families.

We got the police to the bus station as quick as we possibly could.[4]

This was the Birmingham in which, two years later, was to occur the most impressive use of nonviolent resistance in American history.

The Ideology of the Agitators

Simply expressed, the agitator's objective was full equality of Negroes with whites. The grievances of Negro Americans had been aggravated by a century of virtual inaction by the establishment. Later, Dr. King expressed this grievance elegantly in his famous "I Have a Dream" speech:

But one hundred years [after the Emancipation Proclamation] the Negro still is not free. One hundred years later, the life of the Negro is still sadly crippled by the manacles of segregation and the chains of discrimination. One hundred years later, the Negro lives on a lonely island of poverty in the midst of a vast ocean of material prosperity. One hundred years later the Negro is still languished in the corners of American society and finds himself an exile in his own land.[5]

Until the 1963 demonstrations in Birmingham, nonviolent resistance had aimed at quite limited goals. Instances of what Arthur I. Waskow calls "creative disorder"[6] had been confined to specific activities for specific ends. A lunch-counter sit-in, whatever its symbolic power might be, was likely to be instrumental only in desegregating the target lunch counter.

The ideology of the Birmingham agitation incorporated more substantial goals. Bayard Rustin, an important ideologist of the civil rights movement, summarized the goals of the black community in Birmingham:

The package deal is the new demand. The black community is not prepared to engage in a series of costly battles—first for jobs, then decent housing, then integrated schools, etc., etc. The fact that there is a power elite which makes the decisions is now clearly understood. The Negro has learned that, through economic and mass pressures, this elite can be made to submit step by step. Now he demands unconditional surrender.[7]

According to Dr. King, the agitators grouped their goals into four categories. In Birmingham, where only "the bus station, the train station and the airport"[8] were integrated, and those only after violent suppression, the agitators demanded:

1. The desegregation of lunch counters, rest rooms, fitting rooms and drinking fountains in variety and department stores.
2. The upgrading and hiring of Negroes on a nondiscriminatory basis throughout the business and industrial community of Birmingham.
3. The dropping of all charges against jailed demonstrators.
4. The creation of a biracial committee to work out a timetable for desegregation in other areas of Birmingham life.[9]

Hence the agitators' goals were partly economic and partly political, partly short-term and partly long-term.

The ideology of the Birmingham agitators comprised more than a statement of goals. It also included a strong commitment to specific means: nonviolent resistance. Dr. King himself, of course, was consistently committed to this strategy by his philosophy. However, he and the other leaders of the Birmingham movement must also have recognized that nonviolence was the only realistic strategy to adopt. The establishment in Birmingham was white. If that establishment were to adjust, the Negro leadership required the cooperation of legitimizers, of whites to whom the establishment could be expected to listen. Sympathetic responses from such legitimizers simply could not be expected if the agitation were violent. Although the commitment to nonviolence was violated occasionally during the late stages of the agitation, we interpret the violent acts of the agitators as expressive of their frustration rather than instrumental to their goals. An overall strategy of violence for the agitators would have made no sense.

The Ideology of the Establishment

For an understanding of the agitation in Birmingham, we need to distinguish two separate but related establishments. The first of these—and the most visible—was the local government. As the establishment controlling political power, it was the target of the principal demonstrations and the ones that met with the most violent suppression.

Typical spokesmen for the political establishment were Birmingham Commissioner of Public Safety Eugene ("Bull") Connor and Alabama Governor George Wallace. These men reflected the dominant values of the white community. The ideology's central value was a strongly internalized commitment to the desirability of segregation. Negroes, according to the ideology, were inherently inferior to whites, and any attempts to break racial barriers would lead to miscegenation and mongrelization of the superior white race. Further, the ideology claimed that the overwhelming majority of Negroes in the South were content with the system of racial accommodation that segregation enforced, and that no disorder would exist were it not for "outside agitators." Their response to demands for integration and equality was NEVER. They intended to substantiate that slogan in Birmingham, where they were fully confident that the fear in the hearts of local Negroes would make successful civil rights agitation impossible. At his inauguration, George Wallace had promised, "Segregation now, segregation tomorrow, segregation forever!"

Leaders like Commissioner Connor and Governor Wallace, did not, of course, speak for all Southerners or even for all Southern whites. In fact, Connor was voted out of office in April 1963, and prior to that had received criticism for his violent handling of civil rights crises even from the *Birmingham News*, which had earlier supported him editorially. Nevertheless, more moderate views were not significantly represented in the central political decisions made by the Birmingham political establishment before 1963.

The attitudes of segregationists are apparent in quotations from representatives of the political establishment. The *New York Times* quotes some typical statements. Watching the arrest of young demonstrators in 1963, Connor said, "Boy, if that's religion, I don't want any.... If you'd ask half of them what freedom means, they couldn't tell you."[10] Birmingham's Mayor Arthur Hanes called those willing to grant the agitators' demands "a bunch of quisling, gutless traitors."[11] Hanes said of Martin Luther King, Jr., that he "is a revolutionary. The nigger King ought to be investigated by the Attorney General." But Hanes had little faith in Attorney General Robert Kennedy, saying about him, "I hope that every drop of blood that's spilled he tastes in his throat, and I hope he chokes on it."[12]

What kind of a status quo did this establishment seek to preserve? Birmingham was a strictly segregated society. Whites occupied all positions of even moderate civic and economic power. The police force was all white. The city administration was all white. City facilities, including parks, were segregated. Of 80,000 registered voters in Birmingham, only 10,000 were Negroes, though Negroes constituted 40% of the population.

The system was enforced by the free use of intimidation and coercive power. Crimes against the persons and property of Negroes were virtually certain to go unsolved, and the police were likely to turn the other way when Negroes were abused. Not a single bombing directed against Negroes— of the 50 that occurred between World War II and 1963—had resulted in arrests and convictions. Seventeen of these bombings were between 1957 and 1963.[13] Charles Morgan, Jr., a young Birmingham lawyer, said in a speech in Birmingham on September 16, 1963, the day after a bombing had killed four little Negro girls while they were attending Sunday school:

> There are no Negro policemen; there are no Negro sheriff's deputies. Few Negroes have served on juries. Few have been allowed to vote, few have been allowed to accept responsibility, or granted even a simple part to play in the administration of justice. Do not misunderstand me. It is not that I think that white policemen had anything whatsoever to do with the killing of these children or previous bombings. It's just that Negroes who see the all-white police force must think in terms of its failure to prevent or solve the bombings and think perhaps Negroes would have worked a little bit harder.[14]

The second establishment in Birmingham relevant to the agitation was the business community. This establishment was resistant to the demands of the agitators, but not intransigent. It was mainly the business establishment that was to put into effect the adjustments that the agitation eventually produced.

The ideology of the business establishment naturally placed a high value on law and order, especially insofar as law and order led to the preservation and enhancement of property. Business leaders had no particular stake in segregation or integration, but they had a huge stake in the economic health of Birmingham. In spite of their resistance to change, one might have expected the city's economic leaders to have been sympathetic to integration, for most of them were important parts of Northern-based companies, notably United States Steel. As James Reston wrote, the city's "commercial and industrial ties . . . run to New York and Pittsburgh rather than to Atlanta or New Orleans."[15]

Birmingham's agitators, then, were faced with two separate but compatible ideologies supportive of the status quo. One was strongly committed, as part of its value system, to the continuation of segregation and to the enforcement of it by coercive power in Birmingham. The other had no particular value stake in segregation, but strongly desired continuation of law and order, which it saw as most likely to be assured by continuation of the status quo, for the protection of business.

Petition and Avoidance

The organization directed by Dr. King—the Southern Christian Leadership Conference (SCLC)—had many affiliates in the South. One of these was the Alabama Christian Movement for Human Rights (ACHR) which had been operating since 1956 under the leadership of Rev. Fred Shuttlesworth.

ACHR had made several attempts to change the racial climate of Birmingham. Efforts to negotiate with the political establishment failed totally, the establishment being represented especially by Mayor Arthur Hanes and Safety Commissioner Connor. Rev. Shuttlesworth and the organization saw more hope—though it was dim—in negotiation with the business establishment. Several sit-ins had been staged before 1962, but they had been ineffective.

The national convention of the parent organization, SCLC, was scheduled to be held in Birmingham in September 1962. Apparently the planning of the conference included some tentative discussion of the possibility of nonviolent resistance in that city by the delegates and their Birmingham colleagues.[16] At least, rumors to that effect reached the white establishment in Birmingham.

The impending SCLC convention gave Rev. Shuttlesworth additional bargaining leverage in Birmingham, and the business establishment, represented by the Senior Citizens Committee, entered into negotiations with him and other representatives of the Birmingham Negro community. These negotiations resulted in some concessions. "As a first step," wrote Dr. King, "some of the merchants agreed to join in a suit with ACHR to seek nullification of city ordinances forbidding integration at lunch counters."[17]

Shortly after the convention, these agreements were ignored by the business establishment. The adjustment had apparently been made only temporarily, under the threat of a demonstration campaign by SCLC. Actually, it had been part of a strategy of avoidance. Whether the merchants themselves decided to restore Jim Crowism or whether they did so under pressure from the political establishment is uncertain. SCLC decided to act.

Promulgation and Solidification

As in all SCLC campaigns, once the commitment to nonviolent resistance
had been made, prospective agitators went through a period of what Dr.
King called "self-purification."[18] Leaders held a series of meetings at
which it was decided that the principal thrust of the resistance should be
an economic boycott, but that the boycott would be accompanied by
many other forms of protest, including sit-ins and political marches on
government buildings. Because the thrust of the resistance was economic,
SCLC elected to hold the demonstrations during the boom Easter-shopping season. Easter in 1963 occurred on April 14.

In preparation for the demonstrations, fund-raising (for bail money)
was carried out, and other national civil rights organizations were alerted.
SCLC held many meetings in Birmingham, at first concentrating on adults,
later on young people. At the meetings, training sessions would be used
in which prospective agitators would confront each other, one playing the
role of a representative of the establishment, the other the role of nonviolent resister. A principal solidification tactic was the extensive use of
freedom songs. Dr. King wrote:

> In a sense the freedom songs are the soul of the movement. They are more
> than just incantations of clever phrases designed to invigorate a campaign;
> they are as old as the history of the Negro in America. They are ... the
> sorrow songs, the shouts for joy, the battle hymns and the anthems of our
> movement.[19]

A number of the songs stressed the "black and white together" theme.

Later, during the agitation, SCLC faced another serious solidification
problem. This was at least partly the result of a complicated political
situation in Birmingham.

In November 1962, Birmingham voters in a special election had decided to change the form of the city government. This change would
have as one effect the expulsion from office of the incumbent administration, including Commissioner Connor, before their terms had ended. The
administration took its case to court, contending that the incumbents
should remain in power until their terms ended in 1965.

On March 5, 1963, a little more than a month before Easter, a may-
oralty election was held under the new form of government. Three can-
didates, including Connor, ran for the office, and none won a decisive
victory. Therefore, a run-off election was scheduled for April 2 between
the two leading vote-getters: Bull Connor and the more moderate Albert

Boutwell. During this period of elections, SCLC postponed its demonstrations, fearing, according to Dr. King, that agitation would result in more votes for Connor.

Boutwell won the election on April 2, though the old commissioners, including Connor, continued in office while their suit was pending. Boutwell was scheduled to take office on April 15. Within four days after the April 2 election, SCLC had begun its nonviolent demonstrations. The mass media covered them fully.

Almost immediately, besides the usual charge of outside agitation, Dr. King was faced with negative criticism from many who might have been expected to support him. These critics included editorialists from the national news media and many clergymen. Anthony Lewis summarizes the charges:

> A group of eight white church leaders, representing the three major faiths, issued a statement calling the street demonstrations "unwise and untimely," indicating that they should cease in anticipation of the "days of new hope" that would presumably follow upon the swearing in of the new city administration.[20]

Dr. King replied to the charges in his "Letter from Birmingham City Jail," a masterful rhetorical effort, on April 16. In the letter, he recounted the long history of segregation, unsuccessful negotiation, and broken agreements in Birmingham. He stressed the desirability of holding the demonstrations during the Easter-shopping season. He gave strong evidence that the new administration, although it might be more likely to make concessions than the old, would do so only under the pressure of demonstrations. "We know through painful experience," he wrote, "that freedom is never voluntarily given by the oppressor; it must be demanded by the oppressed."[21] He vividly described the psychology of segregation from the point of view of those segregated against. And, mixing example with generalization, he explained the philosophy that required him to violate unjust laws while insisting on obedience to just laws.

The letter accomplished its purpose of solidification among the agitators as well as conversion of many in the liberal establishment. Whether or not Dr. King explained his motives fully can never be known with certainty. The argument that he actually desired a direct confrontation with the Hanes-Connor arch-segregationist political establishment is plausible. At any rate, the old administration did not lose its court suit until May 16 and did not leave office until May 23, almost two weeks after the agitation had ended.

Nonviolent Resistance and Nonviolent Suppression

The agitation began almost immediately after the run-off election of April 2. By April 6, about 35 arrests had occurred, mostly as the result of lunch-counter sit-ins. Then the marches and various other forms of resistance began. On April 6, 42 demonstrators were arrested in a march on city hall. Meanwhile, the agitators were staging kneel-ins at the churches, sit-ins at the city library, and a march on the county building, to demonstrate the need for voter registration. On April 10, Dr. King, for the first time in his career as an agitator, violated a court order to cease the demonstrations. By April 11, between 300 and 400 demonstrators had been arrested, and SCLC had run out of bail money.

On April 12, Good Friday, as he had promised earlier, Dr. King, together with Rev. Ralph Abernathy, led an illegal march. They and about 50 others submitted to arrest.

During this early period of the demonstrations, Birmingham police surprised many observers by using the least possible force to arrest demonstrators. The police seemed to be enforcing the law and nothing else.

A plausible explanation for Commissioner Connor's gentleness is a theory of control to which he appeared to subscribe at least temporarily. Earlier, Dr. King had led an agitation in Albany, Georgia. It had ended with an exceptional lack of success. Credit for its control was given to Albany Police Chief Laurie Pritchett. Bradford Lyttle explains the theory:

> The Albany Movement was prevented from achieving its goal of integration by a system of police control that was able to blunt the overwhelming and disruptive effect of demonstrations. Working in close cooperation with the city's segregationist courts, the police arrested the Negro leadership, dispersed crowds with a minimum of violence. When the movement tried to fill Albany's jails, hundreds of Negroes were farmed out to nearby county, state and city prisons. Soon the Movement lost its drive and ceased to be a threat. . . .
>
> Creator of these successful tactics was Albany Police Chief Laurie Pritchett, whose fame as the man who had stopped the Negroes and King spread throughout the country.[22]

It is impossible to specify that Pritchett's gentle law enforcement was responsible for successful control in Albany, though the proposition seems reasonable.[23] Dr. King gives credit to Pritchett for the success of the controlling tactic, but the Albany Movement also had other problems.[24] At any rate, the theory was not to be confirmed in Birmingham, for Connor was unable or unwilling to maintain the nonviolent stance for long.

Nonviolent Resistance and Violent Suppression

During Dr. King's stay in jail, he had received a telephone call from United States Attorney General Robert F. Kennedy. This event, of course, had received wide coverage from the national news media, and for the agitators it served a legitimizing function. By April 20, Dr. King and Rev. Abernathy were out on bond with new resolve to continue the demonstrations until they had achieved some success.

They furthered this resolve by beginning active recruitment among high school and college students. The response to their appeals was overwhelming. Even very small children volunteered. As Dr. King said, for the first time in the history of SCLC they were able to "fill up the jails."[25]

Under the pressure of the young people, Connor ran out of space in jail. On May 2, about 1000 marched and were arrested. Violence did not occur. But on May 3, with the jails nearly full, Connor elected to reduce arrests and increase dispersion. The tools he used were police dogs and fire hoses. The national news media were there in full force. Birmingham became a powerful symbol.

> The police dogs and the fire hoses of Birmingham have become the symbols of the American Negro revolution—as the knout and the Cossacks were symbols of the Russian Revolution. When television showed dogs snapping at human beings, when the fire hoses thrashed and flailed at the women and children, whipping up skirts and pounding at bodies with high pressure streams powerful enough to peel bark off a tree—the entire nation winced as the demonstrators winced.[26]

At the May 3 demonstration, the agitators remained nonviolent in the face of the dogs and the hoses. However, some Negro onlookers threw missiles at the police.

Nonviolent Resistance and Adjustment

The violence in Birmingham triggered action by the United States government. On Saturday, May 4, while the demonstrations continued, an important legitimizer arrived in the person of Burke Marshall, Assistant Attorney General in charge of the Civil Rights Division. That afternoon, apparently fearing that they could not control counterviolence from the Negro community, SCLC leaders called off demonstrations for the rest of the weekend. About 2500 were in jail.

Marshall was faced with the difficult task of establishing communications between the agitators and the establishment. The agitators were, of course, eager to negotiate, but only if the powerful pressure of the demonstrations was permitted to continue. Both the business and the political establishment were also under severe pressure to reach agreement with the agitators. If the local political establishment failed, Governor George Wallace—not a very effective peacemaker in affairs of this kind—was likely to take control of the scene. Businessmen were suffering, not only from the boycott but also from widespread disapproval of events in Birmingham. Telephone calls legitimizing negotiation were received from U.S. Steel President Roger Blough, President John F. Kennedy, Secretary of Defense Robert S. McNamara, and Secretary of the Treasury Douglas Dillon.[27] The *New York Times* later reported:

> The irresistible argument of the pocketbook is making moderate leaders out of businessmen in many parts of the South. Birmingham's reputation for racial tension has cut new plant investment there by more than three-quarters in the last few years. Other cities do not want that kind of record. And businessmen in Birmingham are taking the risk of leadership because they do not want economic delay.[28]

On Monday, May 6, the demonstrations and arrests resumed. Marshall was having some success with the Senior Citizens Committee of the business establishment. Still, the climate was hostile. The political establishment had not conceded, and would not during the remainder of its tenure.

The following day, SCLC leaders apparently received strong assurance that concessions from the Senior Citizens Committee would be forthcoming. They announced the suspension of the demonstrations as of the following day. The political establishment asserted its independence with an instance of token suppression, clapping Dr. King and Rev. Abernathy into jail on that day, but it quickly released them.

The agreement that was to end the agitation was announced on Friday, May 10. The agitators were granted major concessions by the business establishment, though the accord made no commitments for the lame-duck or incoming city administration. The four original demands were dealt with as follows:

> The agreement provided for desegregation, within ninety days, of lunch counters, rest rooms and the like in large downtown stores (the Negroes had sought immediate desegregation); nondiscriminatory hiring and promotion, including specifically the hiring of Negroes as clerks and salesmen in the

stores within sixty days, and the appointment of a fair employment committee; release of all arrested Negroes on bond or personal recognizance (the Negroes had demanded dismissal of all charges); creation of a biracial committee to maintain a "channel of communication" between the races.[29]

This agreement ended the agitation.

Aftermath and Rhetorical Assessment

Those in Birmingham committed to segregation did not accept the agreement gracefully. The short-term aftermath of agitation in Birmingham was exceptionally bloody.

The day after the agreement, May 11, the home of Rev. A.D. King, Martin Luther King's younger brother, was bombed, as was the Gaston Motel, where Dr. King was presumed to be staying. (Actually, he was in another city at the time.) The bombings gave rise to a small-scale riot in Negro areas of Birmingham, with widespread destruction of property in the affected area. Hostility and legal reprisals continued through the summer, even after Connor and the rest of the old administration left office on May 23. Many were injured. The vengeance reached its climax on September 15, when the aforementioned bombing of a church killed four Negro girls attending a Sunday School class.

This violence might not have occurred if Governor Wallace, the ousted Birmingham city officials Hanes and Connor, and others had not continually given speeches exacerbating the tension among segregationists. Wayne Flynt, in his "The Ethics of Democratic Persuasion and the Birmingham Crisis," has skillfully analyzed these speeches.[30] He writes:

> The speeches can be divided into three categories: (1) in the first group irresponsible individuals advocated direct confrontation in emotional and irrational tirades; (2) a second group of more respectable citizens who possessed high ethos with the public used essentially the same irrational arguments, appealing to fear, frustration, and anger; but these speakers did advise against direct action; (3) both groups identified integration with hated external symbols (the Kennedys, Communism, military force). By their appeal to emotion which short-circuited rational judgment, even the more respectable orators unconsciously made the alternative to continued segregation so unacceptable that any method of resistance (even violence) became justified.[31]

Through all the violence, the SCLC declined to resume demonstrations, taking the position that the agreement continued in effect and that the perpetrators of the reprisals had no official standing. Dr. King wrote later that his "preference would have been to resume demonstrations in the wake of the September bombings, and I strongly urged militant action without delay. But some of those in our movement held other views. Against the formidable adversaries we faced, the fullest unity was indispensable, and I yielded."[32]

The strategy of nonviolent resistance apparently has had its intended effect in the long run. The most recent assessment of the situation in Birmingham was made by *Newsweek*:

> It wasn't too long ago when a Birmingham black man could not try on a pair of shoes in a department store, or park in certain public lots, or work behind a sales counter, or appear on a stage with whites. That is all changed now, as are the whites-only policies of the municipal parks, golf courses and swimming pools.... Negroes hold strategic positions on the board of education, the planning commission, the Chamber of Commerce and all the major civic associations.... Six years ago, seven lonely black children were attending previously all-white schools; today the figure is more than 5000. Voter-registration drives have enrolled some 45,000 Negroes—about half those eligible—creating a power bloc that is energetically courted.[33]

Under the leadership of the business establishment and with the cooperation of the political establishment, Birmingham has made considerable progress in adjusting to an ideology of equality.

Chains of causes and effects are difficult to establish in social affairs. The Birmingham agitation makes it clear that the tightrope of nonviolent resistance is a fragile one. Where grievances are severe, and resistance to social change is strong, the nonviolent resister is constantly between the Scylla of inaction or ineffective negotiation and the Charybdis of violence. Both alternatives are unacceptable. The one does nothing to alleviate the grievances. The other results in the side effects of widespread death and destruction when the establishment is strong, or even when it is not so strong.

The agitation in Birmingham accomplished its principal purposes. It reduced the outward manifestations of racial inequality and served as a potent symbol to other cities, especially in the South, of what might happen if no account is taken of the Negro revolution.

Interesting "What would have happened if ... ?" questions can be raised about Birmingham. What would have happened if Connor had not sacrificed his nonviolent stance on May 3? Probably the demonstrations would have continued until the jails were literally filled. At that point, the establishment would have had to either leave the demonstrators alone or disperse them with force. It probably could not have tolerated day after day of massive marches and demonstrations. At some point, given persistence by the agitators, it would have been forced to adjust. That point would have come with less violence if the political establishment had recognized that change was irresistible.

What would have happened if SCLC had not begun its demonstrations until after Connor and his associates left office? Assuming equal recruiting power for the agitators, the outcome as far as Birmingham was concerned probably would have been the same. Connor was only a symbol of the city's political climate. However, as far as the news media and the nation were concerned, the agitation in Birmingham would have been far less dramatic. Birmingham—without Connor, fire hoses, and police dogs—would have been a less successful symbol for agitators.

What would have happened if the Negroes had been a small minority in Birmingham, instead of 40% of the population? Rather clearly, the agitation would have been successfully suppressed by Connor's early tactic of nonviolent law enforcement.

Such questions help to establish the situational limits in which an agitational movement operates. Crucial to the Birmingham demonstrations were the economic power of the protesters themselves and the greater economic power of those reached by the agitators' rhetorical symbols; the size and persistence of the population from which SCLC could draw; the news-media coverage that finally prompted Federal intervention as a response to police violence; and, of course, the commitment of the agitators to nonviolent resistance. Had any of these parameters been different, the nature and outcome of the agitation would have been significantly different. Birmingham bled, but it survived.

Notes to Chapter 6

1. Anthony Lewis and the *New York Times, Portrait of a Decade* (New York: Bantam Books, 1965), pages 60–61; hereafter referred to as *Portrait*

2. *Ibid.*, page 65

3. Gordon E. Misner, "The Response of Police Agencies," *Annals of the American Academy of Political and Social Science*, CCCLXXXII (1969), page 114

4. *Ibid.;* quo'ed from U.S. Commission on Civil Rights, *Report,* Vol. 5: *Justice* (Washington, D.C.: U.S. Government Printing Office, 1961), page 184

5. Martin Luther King, Jr., "I Have a Dream," in Floyd W. Matson (editor), *Voices of Crisis* (New York: Odyssey Press, 1967), page 157

6. Arthur I. Waskow, *From Race Riot to Sit-In: 1919 and the 1960s* (Garden City, N.Y.: Anchor Books, 1966), page 225

7. Bayard Rustin, "The Meaning of Birmingham," *Liberation,* VIII (June 1963), pages 7–9. Reprinted in Francis L. Broderick and August Meier (editors), *Negro Protest Thought in the Twentieth Century* (Indianapolis, Ind.: Bobbs-Merrill, 1965), page 307

8. Martin Luther King, Jr., *Why We Can't Wait* (New York: New American Library, 1964), page 50; hereafter referred to as *Can't Wait*

9. *Ibid.,* pages 102–103

10. *Portrait,* page 159

11. *Portrait,* page 161

12. *Portrait,* page 163

13. *Can't Wait,* page 49

14. *Portrait,* page 175

15. *Portrait,* page 173

16. *Cant' Wait,* page 52

17. *Can't Wait,* page 53

18. Martin Luther King, Jr., *Letter from Birmingham City Jail* (Philadelphia: American Friends Service Committee, 1963); reprinted in Staughton Lynd (editor), *Nonviolence in America: A Documentary History* (Indianapolis, Ind.: Bobbs-Merrill, 1966), page 463

19. *Can't Wait,* page 61

20. *Portrait,* page 156

21. King, *Letter,* page 466

22. Bradford Lyttle, "The Peacewalkers' Struggle in Albany, Georgia," in Staughton Lynd (editor), *op. cit.,* page 363

23. Misner, *op. cit.,* page 118

24. Louis E. Lomax, *The Negro Revolt* (New York: New American Library, 1962), pages 110–111

25. *Can't Wait,* page 98

26. Bayard Rustin, quoted in Misner, *op. cit.,* page 116

27. *Portrait,* page 160

28. *Portrait,* page 164

29. *Portrait,* page 161

30. Wayne Flynt, "The Ethics of Democratic Persuasion and the Birmingham Crisis," *Southern Speech Journal*, XXXV (1969), pages 40—53

31. *Ibid.*, page 42

32. *Can't Wait*, page 115

33. "The Change in Birmingham," *Newsweek*, LXXIV (December 8, 1969), page 79

Chapter seven

THE RHETORIC OF AGITATION AND CONTROL: AN INTERFACE

A valuable theory should generate precise predictions. In this chapter, we propose a theory of the interaction between agitation strategies and control strategies, a theory drawn from our earlier theoretical discussions and case studies.

This theory should have two principal values for the student of agitation and control. (1) It should enable him to make and test predictions about outcomes during specific instances of agitation and control. (2) It should enable him to decide which instances of agitation and control are worth studying, i.e., which instances are likely to yield useful insights and refinements for the theory itself. For example, a student would probably not study The Weatherman's "Rage Days," which occurred in Chicago during November of 1969, whereas the Vietnam protest movement would prove substantive.

In writing the chapter, we proceeded as follows: First, we isolated what we think are three critical variables for agitation and for control. Second, we manipulated on paper each of these variables in combination with all the others to see whether the differences explained what apparently takes place in actual encounters between agitation and control. Since we thought of each variable as having two levels (high and low), we worked with eight possible combinations for agitation and eight for control, or a grid of 64 possible combinations of variables. We shall present this grid in tabular form after the descriptions of the variables below. Third, given our 64 paper-and-pencil encounters between agitation and control, we extracted some theoretical generalizations. These generalizations constitute a system for prediction about instances of agitation and control, and are the principal content of this chapter.

We do not present in the chapter all 64 generalizations, although the scheme makes it possible to do that. Some are uninteresting. For example, an agitation group with initially high actual membership probably does not exist and therefore is not worth pursuing. Actual membership typically becomes high in an agitation group only after petition, promulgation, and other agitative strategies have been employed. Others among the 64 possible combinations can be combined into more powerful generalizations. Whenever we saw that a powerful generalization was possible, we made it.

The Variables

Agitation

The three agitation variables we consider critical are (1) *actual membership,* (2) *potential membership,* and (3) *rhetorical sophistication.*

"Actual membership" means the number of active members in an agitative group. It is always small, initially. However, as the generalizations will show, other variables often make it possible for actual membership to grow. Like all the variables, we think of it as having only two levels: high (relative to control) and low (relative to control).

The potential membership of an agitative group—disregarding strategies adopted by control—depends on two elements: the strength (logical consistency and empirical validity) of its ideology and the number of people in a society susceptible to that ideology.

One component of ideological strength, *logical consistency,* involves the unity and coherence of beliefs within a value system. In other words, it is a measure of the internal validity among beliefs. For example, most university administrators believe that those students who pay their fees and maintain a certain grade-point average are entitled to the rights accorded to the status of a student: i.e., serving on student-faculty committees, representing their class in student government, etc. When a student who is taking only correspondence courses and who is also an avowed agitator is elected to student office, the logical consistency of an administrator is quickly put to the test. The Yippies, on the other hand, appear to have little logical consistency in their belief system.

The other component of ideological strength, *empirical validity*, refers to the external truth or falsity of a group's ideological statements and assertions. Extreme right-wing groups, flying-saucer devotees, end-of-the-world cults, etc., almost always are logically consistent in their documented reasoning. However, the realities of a Communist plot, UFO's, and The Final Day apparently do not exist, and the statements of their groups lack empirical validity. Some people, nonetheless, are susceptible to ideologies having low external validity.

Susceptibility, of course, is determined by a number of social and personal variables which we shall not consider. Hans Toch's *Social Psychology of Social Movements* is an excellent source for such matters. Again, we think of potential membership as being either high or low.

The *rhetorical sophistication* of an agitative group is the extent to which its leadership is cognizant of and able to apply principles such as are found in conventional books on rhetoric and in analyses such as this book provides. This factor, too, we think of as being high or low.

Control

The three control variables most useful to an analysis of this kind are (1) *power*, (2) *strength* (logical consistency and empirical validity) *of ideology*, and (3) *rhetorical sophistication*.

We employ the power variable as a general one, although what we have in mind primarily are the two types of power that can be most easily eroded: referent and expert.

By "strength of ideology," we mean the same for control as for agitation. To the extent that an ideology has logical consistency and empirical validity, it is likely to be impregnable to agitational attack.

Rhetorical sophistication, again, means the extent to which an establishment's leadership is cognizant of and able to apply general rhetorical principles, as well as those specific to agitation and control.

We think of each of these three variables as having only two levels: high and low.

Figure 1 presents the 64 possible combinations of variables, theoretically representing all encounters between agitation and control. Each cell is numbered and the letters in various cells refer to the corresponding generalizations which predict the probable outcome of such an encounter.

CONTROL

AGITATION	High power / High ideology / High sophistication	High power / High ideology / Low sophistication	High power / Low ideology / Low sophistication	Low power / Low ideology / Low sophistication	Low power / Low ideology / High sophistication	Low power / High ideology / High sophistication	Low power / High ideology / Low sophistication	High power / Low ideology / High sophistication
High actual / High potential / High sophistication	1 C, D	2 B	3	4 B	5 C	6 C	7 B	8 C
High actual / High potential / Low sophistication	9 A, C	10 D	11	12	13 A, C	14 A, C	15	16 A, C
High actual / Low potential / Low sophistication	17 A	18	19 D	20	21 A	22 A	23	24 A
Low actual / Low potential / Low sophistication	25 A	26	27	28 D	29 A	30 A	31	32 A
Low actual / Low potential / High sophistication	33 E	34 E	35 E	36 E	37 D, E	38 E	39 E	40 E
Low actual / High potential / High sophistication	41 C	42 B	43 F	44 B	45 C	46 C, D	47 B	48 C
Low actual / High potential / Low sophistication	49 A, C	50	51	52	53 A, C	54 A, C	55 D	56 A, C
High actual / Low potential / High sophistication	57	58	59	60	61	62	63	64 D

FIGURE 1

The Generalizations

A.   By definition, *an agitative group low in rhetorical sophistication uses the strategies of nonviolent resistance, escalation/confrontation, Gandhi and guerrilla or guerrilla prematurely, before the possibilities of petition, promulgation, solidification, and polarization have been exhausted.* This premature agitation attenuates the potential of the agitative group and enhances the power of the establishment.

Recently, for example, the Women's Liberation Front agitated (nonviolently) for free birth control pills on college campuses. Yet, as their own solidification literature pointed out, birth control devices were already available in any drugstore. This fact alone considerably dulled most of their arguments that women were being denied sexual freedom; most college health centers merely avoided any response and the agitation movement dissipated. "Rage Days," as staged by the SDS Weatherman in Chicago, was a violent agitation which was successfully suppressed in large part because the violence was prematurely staged.

Even if the agitative group is high in potential, a rhetorically sophisticated establishment can often successfully avoid (if the agitation is nonviolent) or suppress (if the agitation is violent) such a group. This generalization predicts the outcomes for cells 17, 21, 22, 24, 25, 29, 30, and 32 in Fig. 1, and sometimes (see generalization C) for cells 9, 13, 14, 16, 49, 53, 54, and 56.

B.   By definition, *an establishment low in rhetorical sophistication either avoids excessively (when suppression is impossible, as when the agitative group's strategy has been petition) or suppresses prematurely, and as soon as suppression is possible (in response, for example, to nonviolent resistance).* This excessive avoidance and/or premature suppression, especially if violent, attenuates the power of control and enhances the actual and potential membership of the agitative group.

Our case study of Birmingham illustrates and amplifies this generalization. If the agitators are high in potential membership and high enough in rhetorical sophistication to exploit control's lack of sophistication, the outcome is likely to be capitulation, though the agitation might be protracted and bloody, depending on control's initial power base. This generalization predicts the outcomes for cells 2, 4, 7, 42, 44, and 47 in Fig. 1.

C.   *An establishment high in rhetorical sophistication always adjusts as soon as it perceives that the agitative group is high in potential membership, especially— but not only—when the agitative group's potential is buttressed by rhetorical sophistication.* Most often, control adjusts as a response to the petition strategy, thus avoiding agitation. When it fails to perceive the high potential of an agitative movement, a rhetorically sophisticated establishment uses the strategy of avoidance initially, adjusting as soon as the agitative group's potential becomes clear. Most of the policies of Roosevelt's New Deal, as well as changes brought about by the normal legislative process, can be used to exemplify this generalization. Another instance worth studying in this connection would be the Supreme Court decision in 1954 to desegregate public schools in Topeka. This generalization predicts the outcomes for cells 1, 5, 6, 8, 41, 45, 46, and 48 in the figure, and sometimes (see generalization A) for cells 9, 13, 14, 16, 49, 53, 54, and 56.

D. *Although an establishment sometimes adjusts voluntarily to an agitative group high in potential (see generalization C), it can always successfully avoid or suppress agitative movements when the three variables are balanced between agitation and control.* This is so because the establishment always holds the advantage in legitimate power. For example, if both agitation and control are high in the first two variables but low in rhetorical sophistication, agitation will escalate prematurely and control will suppress prematurely. Both sides will lose power by this exchange, but agitation will lose proportionately more than control will, and the suppression is likely to be successful. This generalization predicts he outcomes for cells 10, 19, 28, 37, 55, and 64 in Fig. 1, and sometimes (see generalization C), for cells 1 and 46.

One could study the events surrounding the Hungarian Revolution in 1956, Biafra, Nat Turner's Slave Revolt, and similar cases to understand why suppression was successful. Also worth further study would be the successful avoidance of groups agitating for land reform in many South American countries, against Apartheid in South Africa, for recognition of Red China, or for Catholic representation in the government of North Ireland.

E. *When the agitative group is low in actual membership, low in potential membership, and high in rhetorical sophistication, control always successfully uses the strategy of avoidance.* A rhetorically sophisticated agitation group always begins with petition. Even an establishment that is rhetorically unsophisticated avoids petition from a group low in potential, since there is virtually no way that the strategy of petition can be suppressed.

Examples of such groups range from the children who ask "Dad, can we buy a pony?" when their family lives in an urban apartment, to such groups as the American Socialist Party or the Prohibition Party after repeal. Because the agitators' ideology has low potential or because few people are susceptible to it, this avoidance is successful. This generalization predicts the outcomes for cells 33 through 40 in Fig. 1.

F. *The most protracted and bloody agitations occur when control is high in power, low in ideological strength, and low in rhetorical sophistication, while the agitators are low in actual membership, high in potential membership, and high in rhetorical sophistication* (cell 43 in Fig. 1). Such a movement is likely to take the following form: (1) Agitation begins with the strategy of petition; control uses avoidance. (2) Agitation uses the strategies of promulgation, solidification, and possibly polarization; control continues to use avoidance. (3) Agitation uses the strategy of nonviolent resistance; control responds with violent suppression, weakening its own power and enhancing agitation's actual membership. (4) Agitation, now higher in actual membership, uses escalation/confrontation; control continues to respond with violent suppression. (5) Agitation continues through the strategies of Gandhi and guerrilla, guerrilla, and revolution, building its membership at every step when control responds with violent suppression. Eventually, the establishment capitulates.

History provides numerous cases of such encounters: the American and French Revolutions, the Union Movement in the United States, the Vietnam protest movement, of which our Chicago case study is a part, the San Francisco State College strike, and, more recently, the protests against the U.S. invasion of Cambodia, resulting in violent suppression at Kent State University and at Jackson State College.

These six generalizations account for the outcomes of encounters between agitation and control in 44 combinations of variables. The other 20 cells are mainly of two types: (1) Some (such as those in which the agitative group is initially high in actual membership) are unlikely to occur. (2) Most of the rest are obvious in their outcomes, given the six generalizations and some common-sense analysis. A few are interesting, and we leave them for the reader to analyze. We recommend especially cells 50, 51, and 52.

Selected Bibliography

Abrahams, Roger D., *Positively Black*, Englewood Cliffs, N.J.: Prentice-Hall, 1970

Anderson, Albert R., and Bernice Prince Biggs, *A Focus on Rebellion*, San Francisco: Chandler Publishing Co., 1962

Anderson, Walt (editor), *The Age of Protest*, Pacific Palisades, Calif.: Goodyear Publishing Co., 1969.

Arendt, Hannah, *On Revolution*, New York: Viking Press, 1965

Auer, J. Jeffery, *The Rhetoric of Our Times*, New York: Appleton-Century-Crofts, 1969

The Autobiography of Malcolm X, with the assistance of Alex Haley, New York: Grove Press, 1964

Bennett, Lerone, Jr., *Confrontation: Black and White*, Chicago: Johnson Publishing Co., 1965

Breitman, George (editor), *Malcolm X Speaks*, New York: Grove Press, 1965

Broderick, Francis L., and August Meier (editors), *Negro Protest Thought in the Twentieth Century*, Indianapolis, Ind.: Bobbs-Merrill, 1965

Burke, Kenneth, *The Philosophy of Literary Form: Studies in Symbolic Action*, New York: Vintage Books, 1957

Canetti, Elias, *Crowds and Power*, translated by Carol Stewart, New York: The Viking Press, 1963

Carmichael, Stokely, and Charles Hamilton, *Black Power: The Politics of Liberation in America*, New York: Random House, 1967

Cleaver, Eldridge, *Soul on Ice*, New York: Dell Publishing Co., 1968

Crowell, George H., *Society Against Itself*, Philadelphia: The Westminster Press, 1968

Duberman, Martin B., *In White America*, Boston: Houghton-Mifflin, 1964

Epstein, Benjamin R., and Arnold Forster, *The Radical Right: Report on the John Birch Society and Its Allies*, New York: Vintage Books, 1967

Feiffer, Jules, *Feiffer on Civil Rights*, New York: Anti-Defamation League of B'nai B'rith, 1966

Feuer, Lewis S., *The Conflict of Generations: The Character and Significance of Student Movements*, New York: Basic Books, 1969

Fishel, Leslie H., Jr., and Benjamin Charles (editors), *The Negro American: A Documentary History*, Glenview, Ill.: Scott, Foresman, 1967

Fisher, Paul L., and Ralph Lowenstein (editors), *Race and the News Media*, New York: Frederick A. Praeger, 1967

Fortas, Abe, *Concerning Dissent and Civil Obedience*, a Signet Broadside, New York: The New American Library, 1968

Fulbright, J. William, *The Arrogance of Power*, New York: Random House, 1967

Garber, Eugene K., and John M. Crossett (editors), *Liberal and Conservative: Issues for College Students*, Glenview, Ill.: Scott, Foresman, 1968

Gleeson, Patrick, *America, Changing. . .*, Columbus, Ohio: Charles E. Merrill, 1968

Glock, Charles Y., and Ellen Siegelman (editors), *Prejudice U.S.A.*, New York: Frederick A. Praeger, 1969

Graham, Hugh Davis, and Ted Robert Gurr, *Violence in America: Historical and Comparative Perspectives*, 2 volumes, A Staff Report to the National Committee on Causes and Prevention of Violence; Washington, D.C.: U.S. Government Printing Office, 1969.

Haiman, Franklyn S., *Freedom of Speech: Issues and Cases*, New York: Random House, 1965

Havens, Murray Clark, *The Challenges to Democracy: Consensus and Extremism in American Politics*, Austin, Texas: University of Texas Press, 1965

Hayden, Tom, *Rebellion in Newark: Official Violence and Ghetto Response;* a Vintage book, New York: Random House, 1967

Hill, Herbert (editor), *Anger and Beyond: The Negro Writer in the United States*, New York: Harper & Row, 1966

Hill, Roy L., *The Rhetoric of Racial Revolt*, Denver, Colorado: The Golden Bell Press, 1964

Hoffer, Eric, *The True Believer: Thoughts on the Nature of Mass Movements*, New York: Harper & Row, 1951

Hoffman, Abbie, *Revolution for the Hell of It*, New York: Dial Press, 1968

Huntress, Keith, *Murder of an American Prophet: Joseph Smith, 1805–1844*, San Francisco: Chandler Publishing Co., 1960

Killian, Lewis M., *The Impossible Revolution? Black Power and the American Dream*, New York: Random House, 1968

———, and Charles Grigg, *Racial Crisis in America: Leadership in Crisis*, Englewood Cliffs, N.J.: Prentice-Hall, 1964

King, Martin Luther, Jr., *Why We Can't Wait*, a Signet book, New York: New American Library, 1963

Lane, Robert E., and David O. Sears, *Public Opinion*, Englewood Cliffs, N.J.: Prentice-Hall, 1964

Larsen, Otto N. (editor), *Violence and the Mass Media*, New York: Harper & Row, 1968

Lavan, George (editor), *Che Guevara Speaks: Selected Speeches and Writings*, New York: Grove Press, 1967

Law and Disorder: The Chicago Convention and Its Aftermath, Chicago: Donald Myrus and Burton Joseph, 1968

le Bon, Gustave, *The Crowd: A Study of the Popular Mind*, New York: The Viking Press, 1960

Lewis, Anthony, *Portrait of a Decade: The Second American Revolution*, New York: Bantam Books, 1965

Levy, Charles J., *Voluntary Servitude: Whites in the Negro Movement*, New York: Appleton-Century-Crofts, 1968

Lincoln, Charles E., *The Black Muslims in America*, Boston: Beacon Press, 1961

Lomas, Charles W., *The Agitator in American Society*, Englewood Cliffs, N.J.: Prentice-Hall, 1968

Lomax, Louis E., *The Negro Revolt*, a Signet book, New York: The New American Library, 1962

Lynd, Staughton (editor), *Nonviolence in America: A Documentary History*, The American Heritage Series, New York: Bobbs-Merrill, 1966

Mailer, Norman, *Miami and the Siege of Chicago: An Informal History of the Republican and Democractic Conventions of 1968*, a Signet book, New York: The New American Library, 1968

Marx, Gary T., *Protest and Prejudice: A Study of Belief in the Black Community*, New York: Harper & Row, 1967

Masotti, Louis H., and Jerome R. Corsi, *Shoot-Out in Cleveland: Black Militants and the Police: July 23, 1968*, Staff Report to the National Commission on Causes and Prevention of Violence; Washington, D.C.: U.S. Government Printing Office, 1969

Miami Report, Report of Miami Study Team on Civil Disturbances to National Commission on the Causes and Prevention of Violence; Washington, D.C.: U.S. Government Printing Office, 1969

Oppenheimer, Martin, and George Lakey, *A Manual for Direct Action*, Chicago: Quadrangle Books, 1965

Orrick, William H., Jr., *Shut It Down! A College in Crisis: San Francisco State College, October, 1968–April, 1969*, A Staff Report to the National Commission on the Causes and Prevention of Violence; Washington, D.C.: U.S. Government Printing Office, 1969

Perrucci, Robert, and Marc Pilisuk (editors), *The Triple Revolution: Social Problems in Depth*, Boston: Little, Brown, 1968

Progress Report of the National Commission on the Causes and Prevention of Violence to President Lyndon B. Johnson, Washington, D.C.: U.S. Government Printing Office, 1969

"Protest in the Sixties," *Annals of the American Academy of Political and Social Science*, CCCLXXXII (March 1969)

Rainwater, Lee, and William L. Yancey (editors), *The Moynihan Report and the Politics of Controversy: A Trans-Action Social Science and Public Policy Report*, Cambridge, Mass.: MIT Press, 1967

Reed, John, *Ten Days that Shook the World*, a Signet book, New York: The New American Library, 1967

Report of the National Advisory Commission on Civil Disorders, New York: Bantam Books, 1968

Rights in Concord: The Response to the Counter-Inaugural Protest Activities in Washington, D.C., January 18—20, 1969, Special Staff Study Submitted by the Task Force on Law and Law Enforcement to the National Commission on the Causes and Prevention of Violence; Washington, D.C.: U.S. Government Printing Office, 1969

Rights in Conflict: The Violent Confrontation of Demonstrators and Police in the Parks and Streets of Chicago During the Week of the Democratic National Convention of 1968, Daniel Walker, director of the Chicago Study Team, New York: Bantam .Books, 1968

Rubenstein, Eli A., "Paradoxes of Student Protests." *American Psychologist* XXIV (February 1969), 133—141

Rubin, Jerry, *Do It!* New York: Simon and Schuster, 1970

Schneir, Walter (editor), *Telling It Like It Was: The Chicago Riots*, a Signet book, New York: The New American Library, 1969

Scott, Robert L., and Wayne Brockriede, *The Rhetoric of Black Power*, New York: Harper & Row, 1969

Skolnick, Jerome, *The Politics of Protest: Violent Aspects of Protest and Confrontation*, A Staff Report to the National Commission on Causes and Prevention of Violence; Washington, D.C.: U.S. Government Printing Office, 1969

Smith, Arthur, L., *Rhetoric of Black Revolution*, Boston: Allyn and Bacon, 1969

Spock, Benjamin, and Mitchell Zimmerman, *Dr. Spock on Vietnam*, a Dell book, New York: Dell Publishing Co., 1968

The Strategy of Confrontation: Chicago and the Democratic National Convention—1968, Chicago: Gunthory-Warren Printing Co., 1968

Thoreau, Henry David, "Civil Disobedience," *Walden and Civil Disobedience*, edited by Owen Thomas, New York: W. W. Norton, 1966

Toch, Hans, *The Social Psychology of Social Movements*, New York: Bobbs-Merrill, 1965

Turner, William W., *The Police Establishment*, New York: Putnam, 1968

Waskow, Arthur I., *From Race Riot to Sit-In: 1919 and the 1960's: A Study in the Connection Between Conflict and Violence*, an Anchor book, Garden City, N.Y.: Doubleday, 1967

Weaver, Gary R., and James H. Weaver (editors), *The University and Revolution*, a Spectrum book, Englewood Cliffs, N.J.: Prentice-Hall, 1969

Wolfgang, Marvin E., and Franco Ferracuti, *The Subculture of Violence: Towards an Integrated Theory in Criminology*, London: Associated Book Publishers, 1967

Zinn, Howard, *Disobedience and Democracy: Nine Fallacies on Law and Order*, New York: Vintage Books, 1968

INDEX